POWERWALKING

POWER-WALKING

by

STEVE REEVES

with
JAMES A. PETERSON, Ph.D.

Introduction by
MATTHEW GUIDRY, Ph.D.
The President's Council on
Physical Fitness and Sports

THE BOBBS-MERRILL COMPANY, INC.
Indianapolis/New York

The assistance and support of the following people helped make this book a reality: Rudy Riska, Miriam Lamb, and Sue Peterson.

—J.P.

The authors and publisher are grateful for permission to reprint the illustrations that appear on pages, 90, 91, 150, and 151 from the following book:

Physiology of Fitness by Dr. Brian J. Sharkey. Human Kinetics, Inc., 1979.

All photographs of Mr. Reeves demonstrating the exercises are by Janeart, Inc.

All outdoor photographs of PowerWalking are by Janis Monaco.

Library of Congress Cataloging in Publication Data

Reeves, Steve.
   Powerwalking.

   1. Walking. 2. Exercise. 3. Physical fitness. I. Title.
RA781.65.R43   613.7'1   81–18184
ISBN 0–672–52713–8 (pbk.)   AACR2

Designed by Jacques Chazaud
Manufactured in the United States of America

Second Printing

*To James Michener and Robert Vavrā.
Without their encouragement this book
would never have been written.*

CONTENTS

INTRODUCTION

People walk for many reasons: for pleasure, to relieve tension, to find solitude, or simply to get from one place to another. Nearly everyone who walks regularly does so, at least in part, because of a conviction that it is good exercise. Often dismissed in the past as being "too easy" to be taken seriously, walking recently has gained new respect as a means of improving physical fitness. Studies show that when done briskly on a regular basis, walking can improve the body's ability to consume oxygen during exertion, lower the resting heart rate, reduce blood pressure, and increase the efficiency of the heart and lungs. It also helps burn excess calories.

If one is to receive the maximum physiological benefit, authorities recommend brisk walking. The pace should be very fast, the distance covered sufficient to bring about physiological improvement. The distance will vary with the individual, but the walking motion must be vigorous. In this book, Steve

Reeves uses the term "PowerWalking" to describe vigorous physical exertion. In the various chapters, he demonstrates how PowerWalking can become an integral part of our daily lives and how it can help us to achieve our ultimate fitness objectives. His methods illustrate how he has used this technique of walking to achieve optimal physical condition. Even though walking is less strenuous than other popular forms of exercise, it can yield comparable results for those who are willing to invest a little extra time. The secret is to walk briskly for a distance of at least two miles in the manner described in this book.

The President's Council on Physical Fitness and Sports promotes physical exercise as a necessary part of our daily lives. Every American should be helped to find satisfaction and enjoyment through regular exercise. Walking can be used to stimulate our interest in broader physical challenges through other sports and recreation.

It is my hope that everyone who reads this book will understand the true meaning and role of walking in a total fitness maintenance program and will be motivated to walk for pleasure and good health. Walking is inexpensive and accessible, and it can be enjoyed individually or in groups. Try it; I think you will be pleased with the results.

Matthew Guidry, Ph.D.
Director, Community Programs
The President's Council on
    Physical Fitness and Sports

POWERWALKING

1

Put Pride in Your Stride

I love the feeling of being fit. I've always felt that a sound human body is one of a person's most precious assets. Like any asset, if you take care of it, more than likely it will take care of you. And that's what PowerWalking is all about — taking care of your body, improving your level of fitness, adding years to your life, and adding life to your years.

The Greeks have a word *areté*. The root of the word "aristocrat," *areté* literally means "to be the best you can be." I've tried living my life by that precept. What a waste it is when people don't make full use of the potential they were born with. Toward that end, I've always been a voracious reader on the subject of fitness and conditioning and an ardent practitioner of physical exercise. For more than forty years, I've trained with weights regularly, jogged, ridden bicycles and horses, and participated in a wide variety of sports and other physical activities.

I've always been dedicated to being physically fit. Over the years I've spent countless hours and energy searching for the ultimate exercise technique—a technique for achieving and maintaining peak physical fitness in the least amount of time and in the safest way possible. PowerWalking was the answer to my search.

Actually, my discovery of PowerWalking as an ideal form of exercise came about rather casually during a time when I was training my Morgan horses. This particular training program involved walking them as briskly as possible on trails. One day I was leading a thirty-mile trail ride from the town of Anza, California, through the mountains and down Coyote Canyon to a horse camp in Borrego Springs. It was very rough terrain, and several members of the group had not ridden for more than two hours at a time and only on level ground. I decided for the

sake of those relatively unconditioned riders and their mounts to conduct this ride cavalry-style: you dismount and walk beside your horse for ten minutes out of each hour. When I called the first halt, got off my horse, and started to walk beside him, I found to my surprise that I had trained him to walk so fast that it was nearly impossible to keep up with him.

I learned that by lengthening my stride and picking up my pace, while swinging my arms in rhythm with my stride and taking in deeper breaths, I was able to keep up with my horse. I also observed that at the end of the ten-minute walk, my horse and I had left the other riders and their mounts far behind. As I stood there waiting for the others to catch up, I reviewed in my mind what I had experienced in that ten-minute walk. I had been breathing more deeply, thus increasing my oxygen intake, and my heartbeat had quickened considerably and remained accelerated. It was a great aerobic exercise!

The next day I was surprised to find that I was not sore from the long ride as I had expected. The brisk walks had increased my circulation so much that no lactic acid had built up in my body.

In the weeks that followed, I experimented with PowerWalking. I learned that if I alternated breathing in for three strides and out for three strides, I had more endurance. I seemed to get the right amount of oxygen at the right times. When walking uphill, I modified my PowerWalking techniques so that I would breathe in for two paces and out for two. I found that rhythmic breathing was vital when PowerWalking. For best results, breathing in a modified yogic fashion seemed to work considerably better than any of the other approaches I tried. This method involved sequential breathing in three stages expanding the abdominal muscles, the rib cage, and the upper chest, in that order.

As a lifelong fitness disciple, I naturally became very excited as a new and highly effective form of exercise continued to evolve before my eyes. For weeks, I spent several hours, almost daily, experimenting with PowerWalking to improve its effectiveness as a conditioning technique.

Eventually, PowerWalking became a combination of six factors:

- Length of stride
- Rhythmic breathing
- Speed of cadence
- Distance traveled
- Degree of incline
- Amount of weight carried

These six factors produce a form of exercise that looks very much like an accentuated brisk walk. PowerWalking is much more than walking fast, however. Coordinating rhythmic breathing and arm movements with long strides, PowerWalking is a method of developing aerobic fitness that will work for everyone, regardless of age or present fitness. I've experienced the results of PowerWalking for more than ten years. It works for me, and it will work for you.

During my days as a movie actor, almost every one of my roles required me to be in top physical condition. Combining a sound diet with a regular exercise program, I was able to maintain both my weight and my muscle tone at an acceptable level. While eating properly required only a strong sense of willpower on my part, exercising often posed problems. I tried running on a regular basis, but frequently suffered from sore knees. Swimming was out, since I didn't have access to a pool. Ordinary walking wasn't intense enough to produce the desired results. In addition, because we were frequently on location and had irregular hours, I needed an exercise program that could be performed almost anywhere in a relatively brief period of time, that required little or no equipment and could be done at a moment's notice. PowerWalking was the answer to my prayers. It satisfied every requirement. As an added bonus, it was completely SAFE. In over ten years of PowerWalking, I've never had an injury that was attributable—either directly or indirectly—to PowerWalking. My physician friends consider it to be the safest form of rigorous exercise they have ever seen.

One of the most graphic examples of how PowerWalking can benefit everyone occurred last year. A couple of weeks after an article about my PowerWalking program appeared in our local newspaper, a man called me, bubbling with enthusiasm. Apparently he had been suffering with arthritis for several years. He said that he had started PowerWalking after he read the article. Almost miraculously, his PowerWalking efforts had practically eliminated the pain in his hips and shoulders and had enabled him to achieve a range of motion in his shoulders that he had not had for over ten years. For the first time in almost six years, he could sleep without the aid of medication. Naturally, he was both thrilled and grateful, and vowed to PowerWalk for the rest of his life.

Another demonstration of the value of PowerWalking was shown to me last summer while I was on vacation in Fayetteville, Arkansas, visiting some friends. I saw a very attractive young woman in shorts and a T-shirt PowerWalking on one of the athletic fields at the University of Arkansas. I couldn't believe my eyes. When she finished her workout and was leaving the track, I asked where she had learned to PowerWalk. She said that she had seen me demonstrate it on "Good Morning America" and that she used it regularly in her interval training. Her routine was to run six sets of 220-yard dashes and use PowerWalking as her interval activity. She preferred PowerWalking to jogging for her interval training, because she found that PowerWalking didn't put as much stress on her joints. In addition, she explained that because PowerWalking worked her leg muscles differently than did running or jogging, she felt she had a greater ability to recover during the interval, making it possible for her to run a faster 220 yards.

A complete explanation on how to PowerWalk is presented in Chapter 4. For best results, some of the six factors that make up PowerWalking are more important than others. The way you combine these components into a single exercise routine will determine the results you achieve. Instructions for the basic and advanced PowerWalking programs are included in Chapters 4 and 9. The program most appropriate to you will depend on your present level of fitness and your fitness goals. Guidelines for evaluating your current fitness level are given in Chapter 6. Once you have chosen the appropriate PowerWalking program, you should periodically review whether or not your program is meeting your needs and your expectations. Chapter 6 tells you how to chart your progress in a PowerWalking program and how to evaluate your results.

WHY POWERWALKING?

I firmly agree with those who, down through the ages, have praised walking as the most natural exercise of all. Two of America's most noted physicians, Kenneth Cooper and Paul Dudley White, both endorse walking as exercise. Dr. Cooper says, "The overwhelming advantage of walking is that it can be done by anyone, anytime, any place. It doesn't even look like exercise. For those who are timid about being conspicuous, this can be a deciding difference." Noted heart specialist Dr. White lists walking's special virtues: "It is the easiest exercise for most individuals, one that can be done without equipment except good shoes, in almost any terrain and weather and into very old age."

Unfortunately, despite its virtues, ordinary walking can develop physical fitness only to a limited degree. While it can improve each of the basic components of fitness (heart-lung capacity, muscular fitness, flexibility, and percentage of body fat), it can only build heart-lung capacity (aerobic fitness) to a limited extent. For this reason, the American Medical Association's Committee on Exercise and Physical Fitness recommends walking briskly, as opposed to merely strolling. I took their recommendation one step further and developed PowerWalking as a logical extension of the brisk walk.

Because PowerWalking focuses on developing the aerobic system by gradually placing an additional demand on the heart and lungs (a principle referred to as "progressive resistance" by fitness experts), it differs greatly from its cousin, ordinary walking. At least four factors distinguish PowerWalking from other types of walking. In the first place, the longer stride required in PowerWalking is more aerobically demanding than the short one used in normal walking. Also, walking at a fast pace requires more energy than the slow cadence of ordinary walking. Walking up a ten percent grade takes considerably more effort than walking on level terrain. Finally, the additional weight carried or strapped to the body in the advanced PowerWalking program further increases the demand on the aerobic system.

THE CHALLENGE

The next and most important step is yours. I can tell you how you can become physically fit. The PowerWalking program will certainly get you into shape in the most efficient and effective way possible. But what I can't give you is the motivation. Motivation is essential for any change, and you have to want that change enough to make the necessary effort. The programs outlined in this book will, however, go a long way toward making exercise pleasurable and healthfully rewarding. So, it's up to you. After all, it's your body, your health, your future. Why not start today? Put pep in your step and pride in your stride, and get started today. *Areté* is the goal and PowerWalking is the way.

Walk, Don't Run

There seem to be almost as many programs promising simple solutions to fitness and health as there are people willing to advance an opinion on the subject. Some programs promise overnight changes in a person's physical condition even though it may be the result of years of neglect. Others claim to require little or no effort and use slogans such as "total fitness in twenty minutes a day"; "think your way to health"; or "miracle drug promotes fitness." Most of these programs have one thing in common: THEY SIMPLY DON'T WORK!

How can you tell which program is best for you? Unfortunately, I can't provide you with a litmus test. Different people have different interests and different needs. Contrary to what the hard-core running gurus say, the world cannot be divided into two camps—people who run and cretins. Some people don't enjoy running. Others, for medical reasons, shouldn't run. This same thing is true for any physical activity — weight training, cycling, swimming, racquetball, and so on. "Different strokes for different folks" certainly applies to sports and fitness programs. The most important thing for you to remember is this: to improve a specific system of the body, you must place a demand on the system. No demand, no improvement! It should be obvious, though, that practically every form of conditioning exercise can be manipulated to produce at least some demand on a particular system of the body. If that's the case, what criteria should you use to evaluate a fitness program? I recommend three: *effectiveness, efficiency,* and *safety.*

Effectiveness means simply that for the time invested, your exercise program should produce maximum results. Anything less than maximum results compromises your goal "to be the best that you can be." For example, if your goal is to lose weight, why play badminton for an hour and burn up approximately 250 calories when you could PowerWalk for an hour and expend over 800 calories? If you want to build up your heart-lung capacity, why play tennis with its frequent bouts of non-intensive activity when you could develop your aerobic system with the continuous exertion in PowerWalking? The obvious answer to both questions is that you should select the most effective activity.

Efficiency means producing the desired result in the least amount of time required. Anything else is time better spent on other activities. Who would be foolish enough to spend sixty minutes doing something that could just as easily, and safely, be accomplished in twenty minutes? If I wanted to travel from my home in San Diego to visit a friend in New York, I could travel by car, airplane, or train. Obviously, all other factors being equal, air would be the most efficient way to travel because I would arrive in the least amount of time. The same analogy is true for exercise. I can spend twenty-five to thirty minutes in the weight room exercising properly and accom-

Effectiveness-Efficiency-Safety Ratings
of Common Sports Activities

Activity	Can be Performed without Special Equipment or Facilities	Effectiveness (develops maximum fitness)	Efficiency (on the average requires less than 30 minutes to play)	Safety (relatively injury-free)
Badminton	No	No	No	Yes
Baseball	No	No	No	Yes
Basketball	No	Yes	No	No
Bowling	No	No	No	Yes
Fencing	No	No	No	Yes
Football	No	Yes	No	No
Gymnastics	No	No	No	Yes
Handball	No	Yes	No	Yes
Ice Hockey	No	No	No	Yes
Ice Skating	No	No	No	Yes
Karate	Yes	No	No	No
PowerWalking	**Yes**	**Yes**	**Yes**	**Yes**
Racquetball	No	Yes	No	Yes
Running	Yes	Yes	Yes	No
Scuba	No	No	No	Yes
Skiing	No	No	No	No
Squash	No	Yes	No	Yes
Swimming	No	Yes	Yes	Yes
Tennis	No	No	No	Yes
Volleyball	No	No	No	Yes
Walking	Yes	No	Yes	Yes
Weight Training	No	No	Yes	Yes

plish as much or more than someone else could in a two-hour workout. The key is understanding the operating principle behind the exercise and not always equating time spent with results achieved. In exercise, more is not always better. For example, twenty minutes of PowerWalking is more aerobically productive than thirty minutes of an average racquetball game.

Of the three criteria for evaluating a fitness program, safety is the most critical. You can achieve less than your potential; you can spend more time than necessary; but you should never

Each time a runner's foot hits the ground, stress equal to three times the body's weight is placed on all the joints.

engage in an activity in which there is a higher than necessary risk of being injured. The possible trade-off is simply not in your best interests. An injury will diminish, and perhaps indefinitely postpone, your efforts to become physically fit.

For safety reasons alone, it is obvious to me that PowerWalking is superior to every activity that claims to develop total

Examining an injury caused by running.

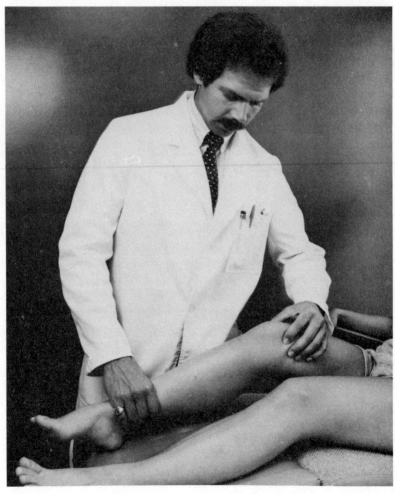

fitness—especially jogging. The list of running-related injuries, for example, is almost endless: knee injuries, shin splints, foot injuries, stress fractures, heel bruises, back problems, muscle pulls, tendonitis, and so on. Is it any wonder that so many people are injured by an activity that so severely jars the joints? It is estimated that every time you put your foot down while running, an effective "jolt" is placed on your body's joints equal to at least three times your body weight. In other words, a 180-pound man who takes approximately 1000 steps while running a mile puts over 540,000 pounds of stress—or *270 tons*—on his body's joints in a *single* mile. Most physicians will readily admit that the human body is simply not constructed to withstand that kind of stress. In response to the vast number of "exercise casualties" produced by the outgrowth of running, there is a new breed of physicians who specialize exclusively in running-related injuries.

PowerWalking, on the other hand, is relatively injury-free when compared with running. You only have to take proper care of your feet in order to avoid the common foot disorders, such as blisters, that may occur when you first undertake an exercise program. Once you've accustomed your feet to the activity, PowerWalking is virtually injury-free. While your body must support the same amount of weight when you PowerWalk a mile as when you jog a mile, there are critical differences in the way you carry your weight. PowerWalking doesn't involve a jolting movement. Instead, you take a smooth progression of steps with one foot remaining on the ground at all times. As a result, there is considerably less force placed on your body's joints, particularly the knees and hips, since the speed at which you transfer your weight from one foot to another is substantially slower than in running and your feet remain closer to the ground.

Surprising as it may seem, some people are willing to take the risk of being injured while jogging simply because they feel that running provides an aerobic benefit that no other exercise can. Obviously, these "true believers" haven't experienced PowerWalking. My next-door neighbor used to be such a person. For months I would meet him in the morning while I was PowerWalking. A regular jogger, he and I often passed each other while exercising. Returning from his jogging session one day, he asked me why I didn't try jogging. I said, "I've tried it. Why don't you try PowerWalking?" He told me that he jogged five miles a day and that he didn't think PowerWalking would give him a good enough aerobic workout.

After several months and many conversations, he at last agreed to meet me at my home one Saturday morning to give PowerWalking a try. I handed him a pair of three-pound hand weights and grabbed a pair of five pounders for myself. We then took off on a three-mile PowerWalk through the hills. He assured me that he wouldn't have any trouble keeping up with me on the walk since he was twenty years younger than I and had been faithfully jogging five miles a day for two years. By the time we returned to my house, it was a different story: his legs were quivering and his complexion had a greenish tinge to it. After a short rest, he recovered. The advanced PowerWalk I had taken him on was more demanding than he had bargained for. Today, this previously skeptical neighbor is one of the most avid PowerWalkers I know.

If I sound like an evangelist for PowerWalking, good! Because that's what I am! PowerWalking will enable you to achieve the greatest level of fitness, require the least amount of time, and permit you to exercise strenuously without being exposed to undue injury. PowerWalking is the near-perfect exercise for everyone, both men and women, from competitive athletes to weekend warriors, and from pre-teens to grandparents. If you want to be totally fit, PowerWalk—don't run—to the starting line.

It Takes Energy to Move

The human body is a marvelous creation. The complexities of its makeup and functions fill volumes of anatomy and physiology books. Bones, muscles, ligaments, nerves, organs, and skin all contribute to your movements, reactions, and thoughts. It is an almost miraculous network that makes these functions possible. In this chapter we'll take a look at PowerWalking and the basic physiology of energy production to show why PowerWalking is beneficial for everyone in your family.

ENERGY PRODUCTION

In order for you to make any movement, energy is required. Where does this energy come from? The analogy of an automobile engine will help explain. Starting a car does not draw on much of the fuel in the gas tank. The starter gets the engine going by calling on the battery for the necessary boost. Yet this power source will not last very long. The engine must begin to use the gas stored in the tank as its primary source of power. And it can keep running only as long as this fuel lasts.

Now compare this with a simplified view of your body's energy production system. Your body has a source of energy stored in your muscles in the form of glycogen. Glycogen produces energy most efficiently when combined with oxygen—*aerobically*. But this combination is not instantaneous. In order to get started in an activity, your body must produce some energy without the benefit of oxygen—*anaerobically*. Once the aerobic system comes into play, it will be the primary source of energy only as long as the intensity of the activity remains low enough so that your respiratory system can provide sufficient oxygen. The limiting factor is the amount of fuel (glucose) available for use in the muscles involved in the activity.

In order to get the glucose to your muscles, you must feed your body. There are three basic foodstuffs—fats, proteins, and carbohydrates. Fats produce twice as much energy per mole (unit) as do carbohydrates or proteins. But fats are much harder for the body to use, or metabolize. Generally speaking, fats are used for energy only during activities of low intensity such as sitting or sleeping. For high-intensity activities, such as advanced PowerWalking, fats are used for fuel only after the body's supply of carbohydrates has been almost completely exhausted. Chapter 7 discusses the role of nutrition and physical activity in greater detail.

Proteins are the building blocks of your body. Their main function involves the regeneration of tissue. As a source of energy (fuel), proteins are used only in a starvation situation. This is because protein, meat for example, takes from ten to twelve hours to digest. During this time, blood is diverted to the stomach to aid in the digestive process. Normally, this is so insignificant that you don't even notice it. During exercise, however, such diverted blood can be more profitably used by the functioning muscles. As a result, eating meats and other protein-heavy or fatty foods before doing vigorous exercise may put unnecessary strain on your body.

Carbohydrates are the most important food source for producing the energy required for high-intensity activity. Carbohydrates in the form of sugars and starches are eventually broken down into a simple form of sugar called glucose and stored in the cells of muscles as glycogen. The storage capability of the muscles can be increased by placing an increased demand (stress) on them. For the competitive athlete this is one of the major goals of his or her conditioning program. In order to increase the amount of energy stored in your muscles, do *not* increase the amount of carbohydrates you eat. For the average person of any age, a balanced diet would include approximately 50 to 55 percent carbohydrates, 15 to 20 percent proteins, and 25 to 30 percent fats. All carbohydrates you eat in excess of these basic percentages, which the body cannot store as glycogen, will be stored as fat where it will remain until needed. The best approach to take if you're trying to build up your body's energy stores is to continue to increase the level of demand placed on your body. This in turn will result in greater efficiency of your energy production system and in a larger capacity for storing glucose.

The next question is, How can the glucose be released to provide the energy needed for PowerWalking? For general purposes, you need only be concerned with energy produced by the two basic systems we mentioned earlier, the aerobic and anaerobic. All of the various types of exercise use a combination of energy from these two systems, although in different proportions. It is incorrect to think of any exercise — including PowerWalking — as strictly either aerobic or anaerobic. For example, when you exert yourself for relatively short distances such as running the 100- and 200-meter dashes, your body is required to convert its energy stores, or glucose, to energy in the absence of an adequate amount of oxygen. In other words, this conversion is accomplished primarily by the anaerobic system. Unfortunately, the anaerobic system is relatively inefficient compared to the aerobic system and is severely limited by the build-up of waste products, which require oxygen for removal.

Theoretically, you could PowerWalk 50 yards without taking a breath, since all the energy required is released before the *aerobic* system contributes. Obviously, you would not think of PowerWalking any great distance without breathing. The oxygen in the air you breathe is essential for the continued production of energy. Air is approximately 20 percent oxygen. After you take air in through your mouth and into your lungs, the oxygen is removed from the air by your lungs and attached to certain molecules in your blood called hemoglobin (red blood cells). The oxygen is then transported by the blood to active muscles where it combines with glucose and releases energy. There are by-products of this reaction which include carbon dioxide and water. The efficiency of this system depends on how well your body can breathe in the air, separate the oxygen in the lungs, transfer the oxygen from the lungs to the bloodstream, transport it to the muscles, transfer the oxygen from the blood to the muscles, use it to produce energy, and carry the waste products such as CO_2 back to the lungs where they are exhaled. Continued stress on the aerobic system is measured by the amount of oxygen that can be utilized by the body during a given period of time. Such a measure is frequently expressed by fitness experts as VO_2 max. VO_2 max is usually measured in milliliters of oxygen per minute per kilogram of body weight. In general, the higher a person's capacity to supply oxygen to the muscles and to utilize that oxygen once it gets there, the higher the level of fitness. The top male world-class runners average a VO_2 max in the high 70s or low 80s, while the top female world-class runners are in the high

60s to low 70s. On the other end of the scale, sedentary individuals and older, inactive people may score in the low 20s. The average male college student scores 44 to 48, while the average female college student scores 37 to 41.

THE PHYSIOLOGICAL EFFECTS
OF POWERWALKING

Now we're ready to look at the beneficial effects of Power-Walking on the component parts of your body's energy production system.

Heart. Similar to all muscles, the heart's reaction to accelerated activity is to increase in size during the activity. This increase results in stronger contractions, which in turn increase the amount of blood pumped out with each stroke (stroke volume). Because more blood is now available with each beat, the resting heart rate lowers. The advantage of a lower resting heart rate can be seen in the following calculation. A resting heart rate of 50 per minute is not uncommon in a fairly well trained adult male, whereas a resting heart rate of 75 is not uncommon in his untrained counterpart. This extra 25 beats per minute translates to 36,000 extra beats per day, and in one year, the heart of an individual with a higher resting heart rate will beat an extra 13,140,000 times. And that doesn't count leap years! The heart, like any other machine, can certainly be expected to last longer with less use. In answer to those people who may say that the difference will be made up with the higher rates attained during strenuous workouts, look at the following figures. With four 30-minute workouts per week, the person with a resting pulse of 50 would have to raise the heart rate to well over 2000* beats per minute, which is ten times

---

*A layman's guide to max heart rate is: 220 minus the individual's age in years. For example, the theoretical max heart rate of a 35-year-old individual is $220 - 35 = 185$.

higher than is physically possible, to equal the 13,140,000 extra beats.

The table that follows presents maximum heart rates, target heart rates, and target heart rate ranges for people between the ages of 20 and 70. Target heart rate range is analogous to your desired "training zone." It is important because it indicates the degree of intensity that you must achieve while exercising if significant changes in your level of aerobic fitness are to occur. You have an upper limit for your target heart rate because if your training becomes too intense (if your heart rate is too high), your exercise becomes primarily anaerobic. In other words, you are not using oxygen and are not improving your aerobic system. In time, you won't need to calculate your heart rate and determine your target heart rate range. You'll know when you're exercising in your "training zone." For me, the

Heart Rates

Age	Maximum Heart Rate (beats per minute)	Target Heart Rate (75% of the maximum in beats per minute)	Target Heart Rate Range (between 70% and 85% of the maximum in beats per minute)
20	200	150	140–170
25	195	146	137–166
30	190	142	133–162
35	185	139	130–157
40	180	135	126–153
45	175	131	123–149
50	170	127	119–145
55	165	124	116–140
60	160	120	112–136
65	155	116	109–132
70	150	112	105–128

target heart rate zone was a good place to start. Now, I get "high" on PowerWalking. I know I'm in my training zone.

Lungs. As a result of a regular program of vigorous exercise such as PowerWalking, your lungs will increase their strength, endurance, and capacity for work. The internal lung volume will increase, creating greater surface areas for the exchange of gases—breathing in oxygen and breathing out carbon dioxide. This increases the number of alveoli used and results in more efficient exchange of oxygen and carbon dioxide. There will be a reduction in the breathing rate during rest, and smaller increases during exercise. In the case of children, it has been shown that their vital lung capacity can be influenced by regular exercise through their growth years.

Capillaries. Oxygen is unloaded in the capillary beds in the muscles. The effects of PowerWalking produce an increase in the number and size of these capillary beds in both the lungs and muscles. This further improves the exchange of gases.

Blood. Proper exercise, such as PowerWalking, increases the stroke volume of your heart along with the number of red blood cells per unit of whole blood. This in turn increases the blood's oxygen-carrying capacity.

Muscle Glycogen Stores. As I mentioned earlier, placing stress on your muscles increases their capacity to store glycogen. Accordingly, your energy stores are expanded.

In general, PowerWalking improves all elements of the energy production system, but the different intensities and forms of PowerWalking I will discuss in Chapters 4 and 9 have varying influences on the system's components. This is why *specificity* is such a key term. Specificity means selecting an activity and an intensity for that activity which will produce the desired results. As you become more physically fit, you should progress to more advanced, intense bouts of PowerWalking. I will show you how to choose the proper PowerWalking program for you and how to modify or intensify it as you go.

PHYSIOLOGICAL DIFFERENCES
BETWEEN MEN AND WOMEN

The physiology of the aerobic energy system includes several factors that help to explain why a man generally should be expected to PowerWalk at a higher level of efficiency than a woman. First, a man usually has greater lung volume than a woman. As a result, a man can take in more air per breath, and thus has more oxygen present in the lungs to begin the aerobic process. Second, a man has greater heart volume, resulting in more blood being pumped per unit of time. Not only are a man's heart and lungs larger, but also their weight relative to total body weight is greater. Third, a man therefore has a greater number of red blood cells and more hemoglobin per unit of blood than a woman. Fourth, the ability of a man's lungs to pass the oxygen from the lungs to the bloodstream is greater; therefore, he can transport more oxygen from the lungs to the muscles. Fifth, research has shown that men have greater aerobic capacities than women. This means that, all things being equal, a man would be able to provide the oxygen necessary for the muscles to continue working for longer periods of time. Remember VO_2 max? Finally, a man has a greater tolerance for handling temperature increases. Researchers have found that women have higher body temperatures at rest than men. In addition, they have fewer sweat glands, lower sweat production, and they begin perspiring at higher temperatures than men. A woman's greater amount of adipose tissue insulates her body, further hindering the dissipation of heat. A woman exercising in a hot environment, therefore, is going to have to make a greater effort than a man exercising under similar conditions. This information is not intended to discourage women from PowerWalking. On the contrary, PowerWalking is as enjoyable and beneficial an activity for women as for men. As I've said, there is a PowerWalking program suited for each person's needs. *PowerWalking is for everyone*!

One Step
at a Time

owerWalking is a progressive exercise. One of its biggest advantages is that you can initiate a Power-Walking program regardless of your current level of physical fitness (with a few exceptions), and gradually increase the level of demand you place on yourself. It is a cyclical process. As the demand increases, your fitness level will improve. At the same time as your fitness level improves, you will be able to increase the intensity (demand) of your program progressively, and the cycle will start anew. However, as with any new exercise program you begin, it is a good idea to discuss it with your doctor first to make sure that your general physical condition is adequate to the requirements of the program.

Over the years I have repeatedly seen a very positive by-product of this cycle. As you experience the positive results of a PowerWalking program, your interest in the program will heighten. Nothing motivates me as much as positive feedback. When I first started PowerWalking, I experienced gains in my level of physical fitness after only a few sessions. The soreness in my knees subsided. I felt like I had more energy. The tremendous tension I frequently encountered while working on a movie disappeared. In short, I felt great! After only a short period of time, I was sold on PowerWalking. Since then I have tried to sell others on the benefits of this revolutionary aerobic walking technique for developing total physical fitness. My efforts have been a labor of love. PowerWalking worked for me, and it will work for you. All you have to supply is the interest in trying it.

In order to channel your interest into maximum results, you should concentrate on mastering the techniques for Power-Walking correctly. I mentioned in Chapter 1 that the six components of PowerWalking are length of stride, rhythmic breathing, speed of movement, distance traveled, degree of incline, and amount of added weight carried to create resistance. Each aspect is separate but interrelated, and each will contribute to your goal of *areté*, being the best you can be. Your job is to find the right combination of the elements for you. As with cooking, there exists the best recipe for your needs and interests.

HOW TO POWERWALK

Legs. When PowerWalking, the heel-to-toe technique should be used, but not in the traditional sense. The heel of the advancing foot should touch the ground, with your knees slightly bent. As you roll to the flat foot position, straighten your leg and drive it forcefuly to the rear with your buttock muscles. As your front leg is driven back, the opposite leg should be thrust vigorously forward, taking as long a stride as possible. It is important to concentrate on keeping the heel of your driving foot down as long as possible and to push off from your buttocks' muscles, not your toes. At the same time, remember to always *stand tall*. Proper posture is a paramount factor in looking good, as well as feeling good.

Arms. To get the maximum benefits from PowerWalking, swing your arms back and forth in a pendulum motion in op-

Proper heel-to-toe technique.

position to the movement of your legs. Your arms should swing forward to an approximately 45° angle and back to a 30° angle. Your left arm should swing back as your right leg moves forward, and vice versa. Allow your arms to hang in a relaxed manner and don't worry about whether they are bent or

Position for the arms.

Proper form, coordinating

the arms with the legs.

straight. The swinging motion of your arms will assist in increasing the length of your stride and will help to counterbalance the powerful force exerted by your legs.

Stride. As you begin PowerWalking, one of the most important things to remember is to stretch out your stride. A long stride stretches your leg muscles and makes them more flexible. As a result, these muscles look better, work better, and are less susceptible to injuries such as pulls, strains, and tears. I personally feel that a long, springy stride will also help you retain your youthful appearance. As people grow older, they

Length of stride is important.

frequently tend to develop a short, choppy stride—a trait that often gives them an even older appearance. My advice to you, regardless of your age, is simple: look fit, feel fit, be fit, and *stay fit*.

Breathing. Once you have perfected your stride, concentrate on breathing properly. PowerWalking involves controlled deep breathing. The particular form of deep breathing I recommend is rhythmic breathing. The rhythmic breathing technique I have found to work best is to inhale deeply for three strides (right, left, right) and then to exhale forcefully for three strides (left,

The third stage of deep breathing, showing the chest arched and the abdomen drawn in.

right, left). Rhythmic breathing involves air being inhaled in three distinct stages, through the lower lungs first, then the middle lungs, and finally the upper lungs. In my opinion, the stage in which air is drawn from the lower lungs is the most important since most people, unless trained otherwise, are generally shallow breathers who use mostly the upper portion

PowerWalking form shown in full motion.

of their lungs during inspiration. As a result, they use their lower lungs less than either their upper or middle lungs.

In the first phase of the three-stage rhythmic breathing technique, you should attempt to push your abdomen outward. This will enable you to force air to flow into your lower lungs. In the second stage, you should attempt to expand your lower

ribs and middle thorax to bring air into the middle portion of your lungs. The third stage of rhythmic breathing involves arching out your chest and simultaneously drawing in your abdomen to support your lungs. This action will enable you to inspire a maximum amount of air into your upper lungs. When you exhale, air should be forced out in the reverse sequence in which it was drawn: upper chest, rib-cage area, abdominal region. I would like to emphasize that although rhythmic breathing involves three distinct stages, these steps interrelate closely and must flow smoothly from one into another.

Speed. Fortunately, your ability to breathe rhythmically will quickly become automatic, like driving an automobile. The next step is to focus on the speed of your PowerWalk. Initially I recommend that you walk approximately a half mile at a speed that is comfortable for you. Next, progress to a half-mile walk at a brisk pace. Your goal should be to work your time for a half-mile walk down gradually to 8 minutes. Remember not to be overly discouraged if your initial fitness level gives you the impression that you'll never be able to walk a half mile in 8 minutes. You didn't get out of shape overnight, and you won't get back into shape overnight, either. Be patient. You've taken the most critical step—the first step. You've recognized the need to be more physically fit and you've identified the most effective, efficient way of achieving your ultimate goal—by PowerWalking.

Once you can walk a half mile in 8 minutes, start walking a mile. Allow yourself plenty of time. I recommend 20 minutes initially. Gradually, however, increase your speed until you can walk a mile in 12 minutes, which for an individual 5'7'' or taller is the equivalent to moving at 5 miles per hour. When you are walking at a rate of 5 miles per hour, you are doing a pure PowerWalk. For individuals who are 5'6'' or under, the target goal for a pure PowerWalk is one mile in 13½ minutes or less (4½ miles an hour).

Once you can perform a pure PowerWalk, there are three ways you can increase its intensity: PowerWalk longer distances, select a course for walking that has hills, and carry additional weight while PowerWalking. Taken in progression each factor increases the demands on your body's systems. Initially you might use only one of the methods, but eventually you'll be doing all three. To continue to improve you'll need to use all three. What is most important, you'll want to.

Distance. Identifying how far to walk is somewhat arbitrary. Once you can PowerWalk in proper form at an appropriate pace, I recommend that you PowerWalk at least 1½ miles. Such a PowerWalk would require approximately 18 minutes — the mid-point of the amount of time (15 to 20 minutes) physicians state is necessary for aerobic improvement to occur. Any exercise involving less than 15 minutes will not produce a training effect on the heart-lung complex — one of the major goals of any program designed to develop total fitness. Personally, I like to PowerWalk for about 30 minutes at a time. Once you've really experienced PowerWalking and the exhilaration that comes from doing something worthwhile, the feelings of well-being, the improvement in your body's capacity to function, the increase in both physical and mental energy, I am confident that you will share my enthusiasm for this remarkable exercise technique. You'll also find that the recommended minimum time for PowerWalking won't be enough for you. You'll want to do more, and you'll feel good because you did.

Course. Selecting a course where you will PowerWalk gives you a great deal of latitude. Initially you'll want to PowerWalk on a basically level terrain. Eventually, however, it will be in your best interests to PowerWalk on a course that includes hills. Because of the added demand that PowerWalking on a hill places on your aerobic system, you'll be able to increase your level of fitness even further. You should anticipate that

during your initial efforts on a hilly course your pace will probably fall below the 12-minute-per-mile cadence that you were
able to maintain on a level terrain. In time, however, your
body will adapt to the new demands being placed on it, and
you'll be able to resume the 5-mile-per-hour rate of speed.

Weights. Once you reach a level of fitness where you can
PowerWalk at least 1½ miles over a hilly course and maintain

PowerWalking on an uphill grade.

a 5-mile-per-hour pace, the next—and final—step is to carry additional weight while exercising. This step is basically an advanced option for PowerWalkers and will be explained in detail in Chapter 9. At this point, though, it's enough to say that for the ultimate level of progressive resistance, advanced PowerWalkers carry additional weight while exercising. The weight is usually in the form of hand-held weights, weight belts worn around the waist, and ankle weights.

The weight belt, hand weights (two sizes), and ankle weights used for advanced PowerWalking.

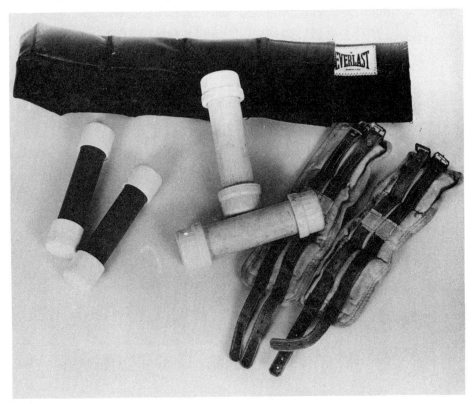

THE BASIC PROGRAM

Although you can devote more time to the program if you wish, PowerWalking requires a minimum of three 15-minute sessions per week. If you PowerWalk only three times a week, the sessions should be performed on alternate days. Personally, I enjoy PowerWalking for 30 minutes at a time at least four times a week. You should structure your program to meet your needs, your interests, and your situation. Try to remember, however, that for you to achieve substantial improvement in your level of total fitness, you must meet the minimum requirements. Anything less will compromise your results. What follows is a sample PowerWalking program for beginners.

Twelve-Week PowerWalking Program for Beginners

Week	Session	Focus	Action (distance/pace)
One	1	•Practice the heel-to-toe technique of walking.	½ mile/slow walk
		•Concentrate on deep breathing.	
		•Remember to maintain proper body alignment, including arm action.	
	2	(Same instructions as for Session 1.)	½ mile/slow walk
	3	(Same instructions as for Session 1.)	½ mile/slow walk

Two	1	•Gradually lenghten your stride. Continue to concentrate on breathing deeply and on maintaining good body alignment and arm action.	½ mile/normal walk
	2	(Same instructions as for Session 1, 2nd week.)	½ mile/normal walk
	3	(Same instructions as for Session 1, 2nd week.)	½ mile/normal walk
Three	1	•Again lengthen the stride. Practice breathing rhythmically. Maintain proper body movements despite the increase in pace.	½ mile/brisk pace
	2	(Same instructions as for Session 1, 3rd week.)	½ mile/brisk pace
	3	(Same instructions as for Session 1, 3rd week.)	½ mile/brisk pace
Four	1	•Maintain long stride. Rhythmic breathing should be coordinated with arm action. Pick up the pace even more.	¾ mile/brisk pace
	2	(Same instructions as for Session 1, 4th week.)	¾ mile/brisk pace
	3	(Same instructions as for Session 1, 4th week.)	¾ mile/brisk pace
Five	1	•Continue as in the 4th week. Again lengthen the stride. Increase distance to 1 mile.	1 mile/brisk pace
	2	(Same instructions as for Session 1, 5th week.)	1 mile/brisk pace
	3	(Same instructions as for Session 1, 5th week.)	1 mile/brisk pace

Six	1	•Alternate walking at a brisk pace (less than 18 minutes a mile) for ¼ mile and then at a fast pace (less than 12 minutes a mile) for ¼ mile. Maintain proper body movements and breathing.	1 mile/alternating brisk and fast paces
	2	(Same instructions as for Session 1, 6th week)	1 mile/alternating brisk and fast paces.
	3	(Same instructions as for Session 1, 6th week)	1 mile/alternating brisk and fast paces.
Seven	1	•Continue as in the 6th week. Stride length should be as for fast pace.	1 mile/alternating brisk and fast paces
	2	(Same instructions as for Session 1, 7th week.)	1 mile/alternating brisk and fast paces
	3	(Same instructions as for Session 1, 7th week.)	1 mile/alternating brisk and fast paces
Eight	1	•Pure PowerWalk pace (5 mph) and proper body movements. Level terrain.	1 mile/minimum pace of 5 mph
	2	(Same instructions as for Session 1, 8th week.)	1 mile/minimum pace of 5 mph
	3	(Same instructions as for Session 1, 8th week.)	1 mile/minimum pace of 5 mph
Nine	1	•Continue as in 6th week. Focus on mobile meditation (refer to Chapter 8). Increase distance to 1½ miles.	1½ miles/minimum pace of 5 mph
	2	(Same instructions as for Session 1, 9th week.)	1½ miles/minimum pace of 5 mph
	3	(Same instructions as for Session 1, 9th week.)	1½ miles/minimum pace of 5 mph

Ten	1	•Pure PowerWalk. Exercise on hilly terrain. Focus on mobile meditation.	1 mile/brisk pace
	2	(Same instructions as for Session 1, 10th week.)	1 mile/brisk pace
	3	(Same instructions as for Session 1, 10th week.)	1 mile/brisk pace
Eleven	1	•Continue as in 10th week. Alternate brisk and fast paces.	1½ miles/alternating brisk and fast paces
	2	(Same instructions as for Session 1, 11th week.)	1½ miles/alternating brisk and fast paces
	3	(Same instructions as for Session 1, 11th week.)	1½ miles/alternating brisk and fast paces
Twelve	1	•Pure PowerWalk. Hilly terrain. Mobile meditate.	1½ miles/minimum pace of 5 mph
	2	(Same instructions as for Session 1, 12th week.)	1½ miles/minimum pace of 5 mph
	3	(Same instructions as for Session 1, 12th week.)	1½ miles/minimum pace of 5 mph

Stretching

Stretching is like using dental floss. When a dentist asks his patient if he has been flossing, the initial response is, "Yes, but not as much as I should." When I question my friends about their stretching program, I get the same reply. It seems that everyone has some idea that stretching is beneficial, but people just can't find sufficient time to work it into their exercise programs. Please excuse the pun, but an adequate level of flexibility is one way of "stretching" out your athletic years. It is owning an insurance policy in case of injury. You are less likely to be injured, and if you do get hurt, the injuries usually take less time to heal.

When I was body building competitively, hardly any mention was made of stretching. I ran to increase my stamina, lifted weights to gain muscle size and strength, but did little to develop flexibility other than to concentrate on performing every exercise through a full range of motion with complete muscle contraction and extension. Over the years, however, because of my deep interest in physical fitness and my extensive reading about various aspects of fitness, I have become a very strong advocate of a proper stretching program. I know of friends who have recovered from various injuries with no treatment other than stretching.

THE PHYSIOLOGY OF STRETCHING

Your joints connect one bone to another. Motion occurs through these joints by way of muscles and their tendons. Your tendons act as pulleys to move these joints. The stress of your body's weight in any physical activity such as PowerWalking is absorbed through these joints much like a shock absorber absorbs the impact of the road on a car. For that reason, it is important that before engaging in any physical activity, you prepare your joints for the jolts that they might subsequently receive. Such preparation involves stretching before exercising.

Stretching before working out does two important things. First, it sends a signal to your muscles that they are about to undergo work. The exertion of PowerWalking will be better tolerated with a more relaxed muscle. Stretching gets the "kinks" out and a smoother "ride" is assured. Second, proper stretching raises the body temperature. Raising the body temperature even one degree before working out decreases the chance of injury. Wearing a sweatsuit or a warmup outfit while stretching will help to raise the body's temperature. Remember not to be overzealous during your warmups. You want to awaken the muscles gradually, not shock them!

Guidelines for Stretching

• Wear loose clothing.

• The objective of each exercise should be to stretch until you feel discomfort and then relax. You want to stretch progressively without pain!

• Perform each exercise in a smooth, steady fashion. Avoid all bouncing and jerking.

• Each exercise should be held a minimum of 6 to 10 seconds per repetition. As your PowerWalks or workouts increase, you can consider increasing the time each repetition is held to a maximum of 20 to 30 seconds.

• Halfway through each exercise, slightly increase the degree of stretch for the remaining time.

• If you PowerWalk or work out in the early morning, perform two sets of each stretching exercise. You are naturally stiffer in the morning than in the evening.

• Don't be overzealous. Some people feel that if they stretch to the point of pain, they will increase their flexibility faster. This is definitely not true. The only thing that comes from this is injury.

• Your "cooling-down" program should include the same exercises as your "warmup" program.

STRETCHING EXERCISES

You can use the following 22 exercises as a general warmup stretching routine. You can use this same routine after Power-Walking for cooling down and to minimize the possibility that your muscles might tighten up.

Begin in a seated position with legs spread (Exercise 1). Bending at the waist, reach toward your right foot with both hands, and try to touch your knee with your forehead. Hold this position for a count of 6. Repeat, reaching toward your left foot. Straighten up and return to the center position. Repeat this entire exercise 3 to 5 times. With each repetition, you should feel yourself stretching farther and more easily. This exercise stretches your hamstrings and lower back.

Exercise 1.

While remaining in a seated position, bring your legs together in front of you (Exercise 2). Reach over and grasp your feet. Extend your ankles, toes pointed away from your body, and try to bring your forehead to your knees by pulling on the soles of your feet. Do this slowly and easily. Hold for a count of 8, return to your starting position. Do this exercise 3 to 5 more times. This exercise is good for stretching your calf muscles.

Exercise 2.

The next exercise helps loosen the frontal thigh muscles (quadriceps). Still seated on the floor, assume a hurdler's position by extending one leg in front of you and bending the other back behind you (Exercise 3). Keeping your extended knee straight, bend forward from the waist and pull your forehead toward your knee. Hold for a count of 6. Return to the starting position. After 4 to 6 repetitions, change over and extend the opposite leg.

Exercise 3.

Now, sit with your knees pointing out to each side and the soles of your feet touching each other and pulled as close to you as possible (Exercise 4). Bend at the waist and try to touch your chest to your feet. This is very difficult, so don't be discouraged if you are only able to bend a short distance. Hold this position for a count of 8. Repeat 6 to 8 times. This exercise is designed to stretch your inner thighs.

Exercise 4.

Exercise 5.

Exercise 5 is designed to stretch the lower back muscles. Lie flat on your back, legs extended and close together. Slowly raise your legs and bring them up over your head, keeping your knees straight, until your toes touch the ground behind you. As you feel the muscles in your lower back begin to stretch, try to move your feet farther away from your head. As your flexibility increases, you may want to take this exercise one step farther by bringing your knees to the ground on either side of your head (Exercise 6). This is a yoga position and requires good breath control.

Exercise 6.

Several abdominal exercises exist that, if properly performed, will strengthen your abdominal muscles. Sit-ups are one of the most common exercises done for these muscles. Lie flat on your back with your knees bent, your feet flat on the ground, and your hands interlocked behind your head (Exercise 7). Now, sit up and touch your elbows to your knees. Then slowly lower yourself to the floor. Repeat this as many times as you can, but try to do at least 15 repetitions.

Exercise 7.

As your abdominal muscles become stronger, you may want to try a more challenging exercise, the curl-up. Lie on your back with your knees bent, feet flat on the floor and hands laced behind your head. This position is the same as for the sit-up except that the hips are elevated by a pillow or a pad (Exercise 8). Curl up slowly, bringing your head toward your knees. As you reach an upright position, immediately begin to lower yourself slowly. Before your head touches the ground, curl up again. At first it may be very difficult to complete three or four repetitions of this exercise. When done properly, however, stress will be exerted on your abdominal muscles in both the curling up and the lowering phases of the exercise. The muscles will be taxed to their limit much more quickly than with conventional sit-ups.

Exercise 8.

Other abdominal strengtheners include leg raise and bicycle exercises. Lie flat on the ground, with your arms at your sides and your legs raised about 12 inches off the ground and held close together. To do the leg raises, slowly open and close your legs while keeping them in the raised position (Exercise 9). Start with 10 to 12 repetitions.

Exercise 9.

Next, pump your legs in a circular motion as if riding a bicycle, keeping them no more than 12 inches off the ground (Exercise 10). Begin with about 30 seconds of this exercise.

Exercise 10.

Other very simple abdominal exercises that you can do almost anywhere are exercises that involve contracting selected muscle groups. One example is to contract your abdominal muscles as much as possible, pulling your navel in toward your spine. Relax. Another exercise involves contracting your buttock muscles as hard as you can. Relax. You can also do both together. Hold each contraction for 15 seconds. Repeat 15 times. These exercises can be done frequently during the day, whenever and wherever you think of them.

The next two exercises require a partner. The first one is designed to increase both flexibility and strength in the ankles. Sit flat on the ground, with your legs extended (Exercise 11). Your partner then rotates your ankles several times through their full range of motion, first in one direction, then in the other.

Exercise 11.

Now, your partner holds your foot near the toes as you first extend the ankle, pushing against the resistance and then flex the ankle, pulling away from the resistance. Still pushing against your partner's hand, turn your ankle inward, and finally turn it outward. Each movement should be performed 6 times in succession before moving on to the next (Exercise 12). This set of exercises feels particularly good after a long run. They help build up the strength and flexibility necessary to reduce the possibility of ankle injuries caused by running on uneven surfaces.

Exercise 12.

Another exercise that requires a partner is one designed to help strengthen your hamstrings. Lie flat on your stomach with your arms at your sides. While your partner applies resistance against the back of your calf, lift your lower leg by bending your knee (Exercise 13). Then lower the leg, also against your partner's resistance. Repeat this exercise 6 to 8 times for each leg.

Exercise 13.

(A)

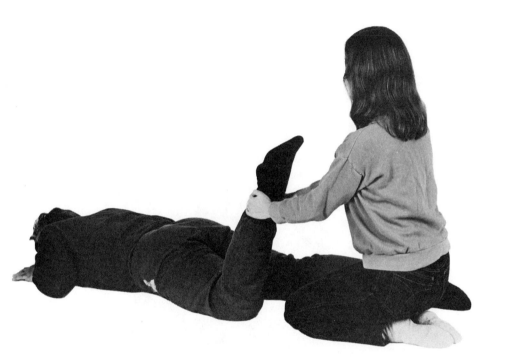

(B)

A number of stretching exercises can be performed in the standing position. For example, stand with your legs together and try to touch your toes by bending at the waist while keeping your knees straight (Exercise 14). Hold for a count of 6 and repeat 4 to 6 times.

Exercise 14.

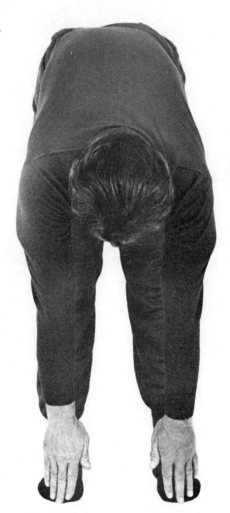

Then place one foot in front of the other and try to touch your toes. Now place the other foot in front and repeat. Alternate feet after each repetition (Exercise 15).

Exercise 15.

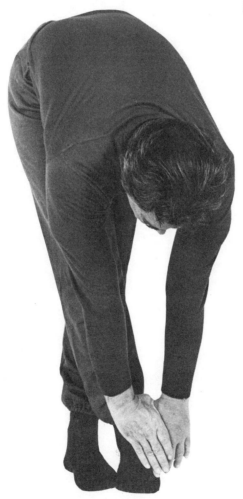

Next, spread your legs, bend at the waist, and using both hands, touch your left foot, then the ground between your feet, and finally your right foot (Exercise 16). Hold each position for a count of 6 and repeat 4 to 6 times.

Exercise 16.

Standing with legs spread, lunge gently to the left and then lunge to the right to stretch the muscles in your groin (Exercise 17). Hold each position for a count of 10 and repeat 4 to 6 times.

Exercise 17.

Exercises 18 and 19 are designed to stretch your calf muscles. Place a thick telephone book on the floor in front of you. With your feet approximately hip-width apart, position the balls of your feet on the book and rise up on your toes. Then rock back onto your heels (Exercise 18).

Exercise 18.

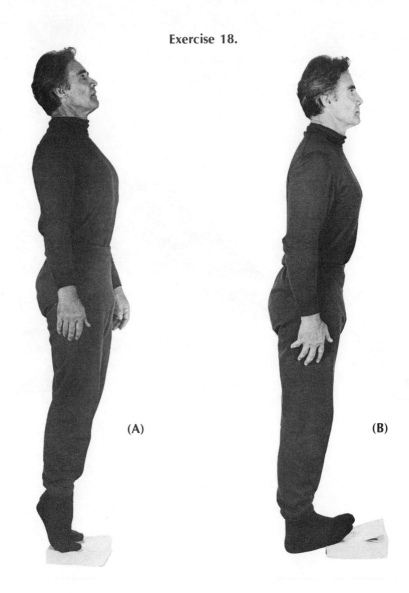

(A)   (B)

Now push against the wall, tree, or any other stationary object with your hands, keeping one leg extended back and the forward leg bent (Exercise 19). Hold this position with the heels flat on the ground for a count of 6. Repeat 4 times for each leg.

This exercise can also be done with both legs extended to the rear. This is sometimes referred to as a wall push-up.

Exercise 19.

Your upper body can be sufficiently limbered up by performing a series of arm circles, shoulder shrugs, and head circles.
Arm circles (Exercise 20) are done by holding your arm straight
out in front of you and rotating it from the shoulder. Make full
circles, first forward, then backward. Exercise one arm at a
time and then both arms together.

Exercise 20.

(A) (B)

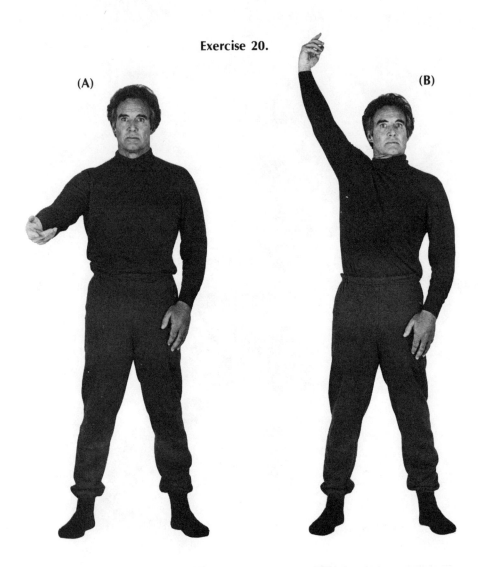

Exercise 21.

(A)

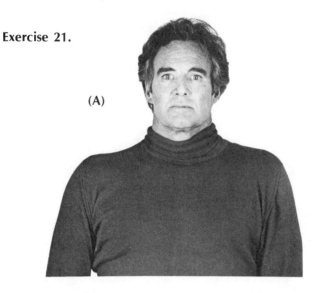

Shoulder shrugs (Exercise 21) are performed by standing with your feet 18 inches apart with your arms at your sides. Raise your shoulders up and then forward and finally down and back.

(B)

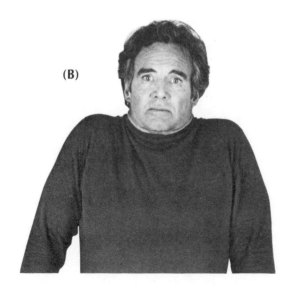

Exercise 22.

(A)

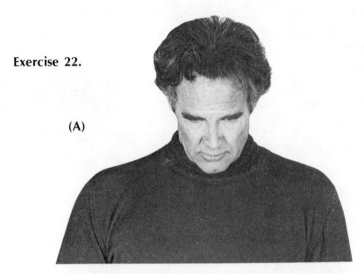

Head circles (Exercise 22) are also performed from a standing position. With your body relaxed, drop your head forward until your chin touches your chest. Slowly circle your head first to the right for approximately 15 seconds, and then to the left, also for 15 seconds. Be your own judge as to how long to perform these exercises. Certainly 30 seconds for each should be sufficient.

(B)

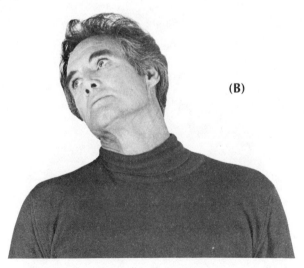

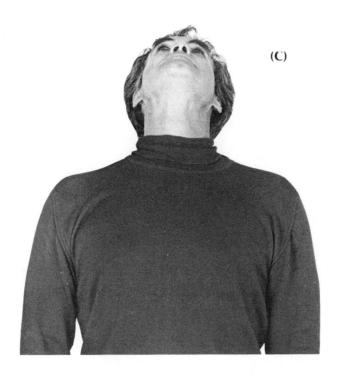

(C)

If you perform all these exercises properly, they should provide you with an extensive stretching regimen for the lower back, legs and upper body. Personally, I find that I usually don't have the time to perform all 22 exercises. In those situations, I try to select at least one exercise for each particular body area. Doing at least one exercise for a specific muscle group will prepare that area for most of the demands it might encounter. My favorite short routine for days when I don't have time to do the full workout includes nine essential exercises that stretch and prepare all parts of the body for action.

MY FAVORITE SHORT WARMUP
AND COOL-DOWN ROUTINE

Begin by placing a 2-inch block or a 2 × 4 on the floor in front of you. With your feet 12 inches apart, position your toes on the block or board, then bend forward from your waist, keeping your knees straight. Try to touch the floor with your fingertips or palms, depending on your flexibility (Exercise 23).

Exercise 23.

Exercise 24.

From a standing position, lunge forward 3 to 4 feet with your right leg. Place your hands on the floor for balance and stretch your left leg back as far as possible, keeping it straight. Repeat again, lunging forward with the left leg (Exercise 24).

Standing with your feet together, bend your right leg at the knee and grasp your foot behind you with your right hand. Pull your leg up until the heel touches the buttock. Balance yourself with your left hand against a wall or tree. Repeat this stretch with the left leg (Exercise 25).

Exercise 25.

Now stand with your feet 18 inches apart with your hands on your hips. Bend forward from the waist until your upper body is parallel to the floor. Return to the upright position (Exercise 26). Repeat 25 times.

Exercise 26.

(A)

(B)

Standing with your feet 18 inches apart, grasp your T-shirt or sweat shirt at chest height, and bend as far to the left as possible. Then bend to the right, keeping your elbows close to your sides (Exercise 27). Repeat 25 times.

(A)

Exercise 27.

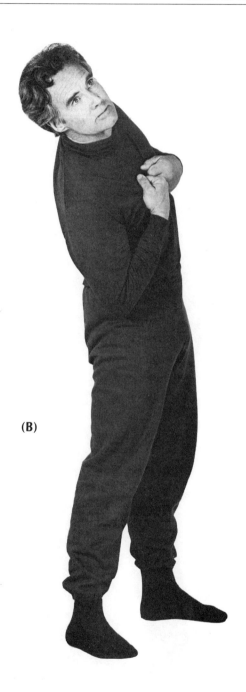

(B)

Now place your hands on your hips and stand with your feet 18 inches apart. Twist only your upper body to the left as far as possible. Don't move from the hips down. Then twist to the right as far as you can (Exercise 28). Repeat 25 times.

(A)

Exercise 28.

(B)

I always end with the arm circles, shoulder shrugs, and head circles described earlier. I'll repeat them here for easier reference. To do arm circles, hold your arm straight out in front of you and rotate it from the shoulder in a full forward circle 15 times, then in a full backward circle 15 times (Exercise 20). Repeat with the other arm, then with both arms together.

Exercise 20.

(A)   (B)

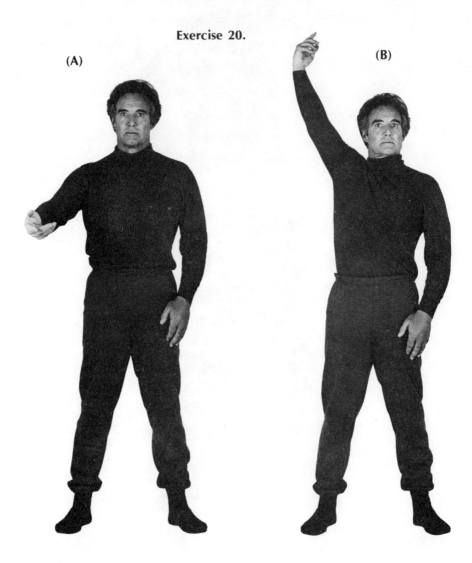

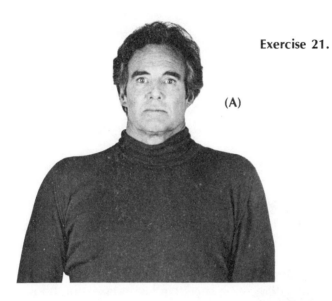

Exercise 21.

(A)

Now standing with your feet 18 inches apart and your arms at your sides, raise your shoulders up and forward, then down and back (Exercise 21).

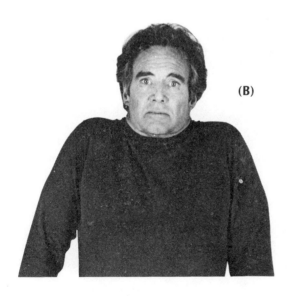

(B)

Exercise 22.

(A)

Finally, to do the head circles, relax your body and drop your head forward until your chin touches your chest. Slowly circle your head first to the right for approximately 15 seconds, and then to the left (Exercise 22). Imagine yourself making giant circles with the top of your head.

(B)

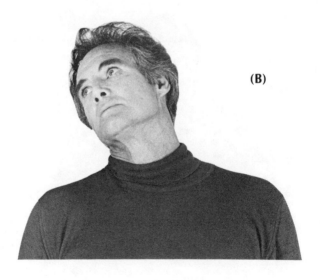

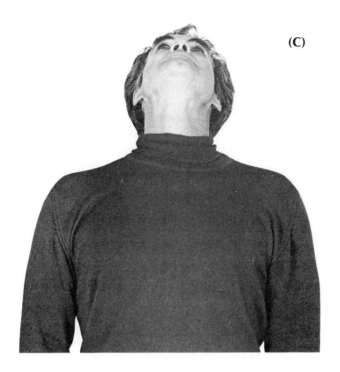

(C)

Even if you do no other exercises before your PowerWalk, you should always do these simple stretching and bending exercises. To get the full benefit of your exercise program it is important to properly warm up and cool down your muscles.

COOLING DOWN

Stretching should be done after workouts, as well. Your muscles have become contracted due to the intensity of the workout and should not be allowed to remain in this shortened state. Many muscle spasms are a direct result of not stretching after exercising strenuously. Proper stretching will also minimize the amount of stress your body will face from the next day's warmup and workout. If you do cool-down exercises, I suggest that you repeat the exercises you did for your warmup program.

DAYS OFF

Even on days that you are not PowerWalking, you should spend a few minutes stretching. Think of it as extra protection. You are giving your muscles a needed stretch without subjecting them to the stress of strenuous exercise. You are a little bit ahead of the game now. This is an inexpensive protective measure that pays off by extending the amount of time you can spend exercising *injury-free*.

Evaluating
and Charting
Your Progress

An effective conditioning program requires proper planning. PowerWalking is certainly no exception. In order for you to achieve maximum results from your program, you need to evaluate how well it is working for you and adjust it accordingly. I recommend that you base this evaluation on whether or not your program is meeting reasonable goals within a reasonable time frame. Obviously, neither PowerWalking nor any other activity can enable you to lose 50 pounds in a week or increase your strength to a Herculean level in a month. What you have to do is to determine your present level of fitness and then, based on the results of that evaluation, set attainable goals for yourself. PowerWalking is a terrific form of exercise for helping you reach your goals. I always try to follow the "3-b rule" whenever setting goals: *be* realistic, *be* patient, and *be*lieve in yourself.

SELF-EVALUATION

Begin by determining how fit you are in each of the following categories: aerobic fitness (cardiovascular functioning),
muscular endurance, strength, flexibility, and body composition. Each component of physical fitness can be tested by
means of simple, nonlaboratory measures.

AEROBIC FITNESS

The most practical nonlaboratory tests of aerobic fitness are
Kenneth H. Cooper's 12-minute field test, and modifications of
what is known as a step test. In Cooper's 12-minute test—
Cooper wrote *Aerobics* and *The New Aerobics*—you are required to walk or run as far as you can in 12 minutes. Based on
your distance over the 12 minutes, you are ranked as having an
excellent, good, average, poor, or very poor level of aerobic
fitness. To be ranked as having excellent aerobic fitness, you
have to walk or run at least 1¾ miles in 12 minutes (slightly
less than a 7-minute-per-mile pace).

I prefer the step test; it is more easily performed, more feasi-
ble for people of different fitness levels, and basically requires
little equipment except for a bench. In the step test, you alter-
nately step up and down on a bench or step that can range in
height from 12 to 20 inches at a specific cadence. The stepping
activity goes on for a specific period of time and your post-
activity heart rate is determined to estimate your body's ability
to recover from the demands placed on your cardiovascular

Step test for aerobic fitness.

system. For the most widely used step test, which comes from Harvard, the following scoring formula has been developed:

$$\text{Physical Efficiency Index (PEI)} = \frac{\text{Duration of exercise in seconds} \times 100}{(5.5) \times \text{your pulse count taken 1 to 1½ minutes after you have finished stepping.}}$$

To determine your PEI rating, first multiply the number of seconds you exercised by 100. Then divide that total by a number determined by multiplying your pulse count (which you should take 60 to 90 seconds after you have finished exercising) by 5.5. If your PEI rating is less than 50, you should

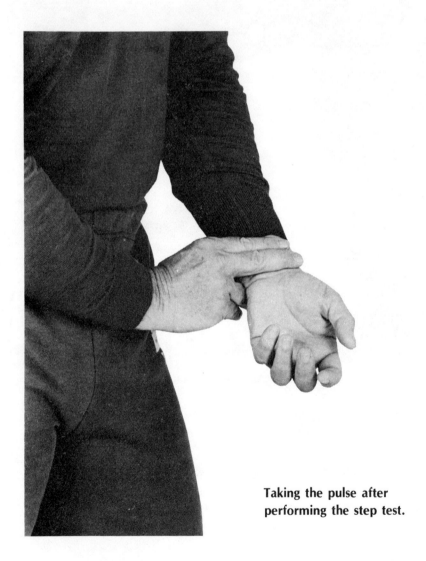

Taking the pulse after performing the step test.

be concerned that your heart-lung level of fitness is less than desirable. If it's higher than 80, you're in an excellent state of aerobic fitness. PEI rankings are given below:

PEI	Ranking
Below 50	Poor
50–80	Average
Above 80	Good

Another widely used and acclaimed step test is one developed by Brian J. Sharkey for the U.S. Forest Service. On Dr. Sharkey's test, you step up and down on a bench (15¾ inches high for men, 13 inches high for women) at a rate of 22½ steps per minute. When 5 minutes of exercise have been completed, you sit down and take your pulse exactly 15 seconds, starting exactly at 15 seconds after exercise and ending exactly at 30 seconds after exercise. Your weight should be taken wearing the clothes you had on during the exercise.

The tables at the end of this chapter present scoring data that will allow you to interpret what your step test results mean. Tables 1 and 2 provide you with a fitness score based on both your post-exercise pulse count and your weight. Tables 3 and 4 offer a fitness score adjusted for age. Since your maximal pulse declines as you get older, it is necessary to adjust your score for age. Finally, Table 5 presents a simple means for you to evaluate your general level of aerobic fitness based on tables of age-adjusted fitness scores.

Regardless of what step test or system of evaluation you use, all testing conditions should be standardized (time, bench height, cadence, length of the test, and so on). Take your pulse by placing your fingers either on the radial pulse (wrist) or on the carotid pulse (slight pressure to the left or right of the Adam's apple).

MUSCULAR ENDURANCE

Muscular endurance is measured by exercising against a resistance representing less than your level of maximal strength. Isotonic (moving as opposed to static or isometric) endurance is usually tested by using your own body weight as the resistance. The most commonly employed endurance tests are pull-ups, chin-ups, push-ups, sit-ups, and dips. Based on data provided by the President's Council on Physical Fitness and Sports and the American Association for Health, Physical Education, and Recreation, the table that follows lists a performance rating for men on these items.

Normative Scale by Selective Muscular Endurance Items

	Pull-ups	Chin-ups	Sit-ups	Push-ups (bent knee)	Dips (1 minute)
Excellent	12+	14+	68+	50+	25+
Good	9–11	10–13	52–67	39–49	18–24
Average	6–8	6–9	36–51	25–38	9–17
Poor	3–5	3–5	29–35	12–24	4–8
Very Poor	0–2	0–2	0–28	0–11	0–3

Note: All scores are for men only; physical fitness testing "experts" have so underestimated the physical capabilities of athletically inclined women that the existing norms for women are apparently highly inaccurate.

STRENGTH

In theory, you can test your level of isotonic (moving) strength by determining how much resistance (weight) one of your given muscle groups can move through the full range of joint motion. In reality, such measurements are somewhat meaningless except as a relative comparison over time. If you can lift a given amount on a specific exercise and that amount is greater than previously lifted using the same equipment for the same exercise, you can argue that you are stronger. Such a change in the amount lifted, however, may be due to the way you performed the exercise or the learning effect (neurological efficiency) as much as to an increase in strength. There simply is no practical way to determine the precise cause of the change. In addition, given the anatomical and neurological differences between individuals, a listing of the numerous norms for the various muscle groups would be virtually useless. One example of such a totally arbitrary norm is that you should be able to standing (military) press a weight equal to at least your own body weight in order to be considered above average. I personally follow what I believe are more practical guidelines when it comes to muscular fitness: Will my muscles enable me to do what I want to do, when I want to do it? Do my muscles afford me maximum protection against the chance of being injured? If the answer to both questions is yes, then I feel that my strength is adequate.

FLEXIBILITY

Evaluating your level of flexibility is somewhat difficult because flexibility is specific to a particular joint. As a result, no single test provides an evaluation of the flexibility of all the major joints of the body. Figures 1 and 2 illustrate the normal range of motion for all of your body's major joints. In terms of measuring overall flexibility, the problem is that you may be flexible in one area of your body and relatively inflexible in another. The flexibility requirements for a healthy lifestyle will also vary slightly from individual to individual. I highly recommend that you try to maintain maximum flexibility in your body's major joints (lower back, hips, knees, and shoulders). PowerWalking, combined with stretching exercises, is an excellent technique for developing the suppleness of your muscles. Chapter 5 outlined several exercises that you might use to

Trunk flexion test.

(A)

augment your program. An example of a commonly used flexibility test is the trunk flexion test. In this test you stand on a box or low platform. Keeping your knees locked, you bend forward at the waist and reach down as far as you can. If you can reach your toes, you score a 0. (A) For every inch above or below your toes, you receive either a minus (above the toes) or a plus (below your toes) score. (B) The average score for college men is +1 and for college women, +4.

(B)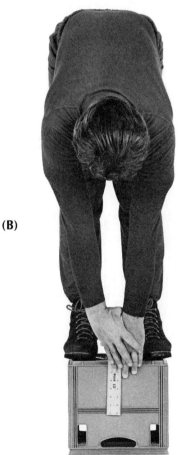

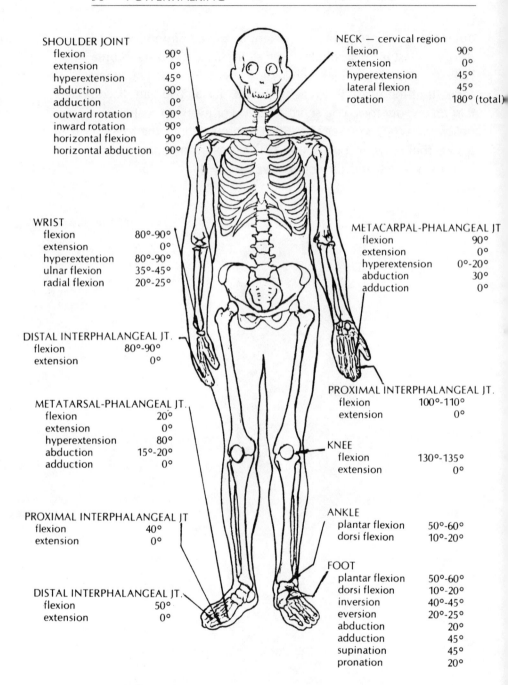

SHOULDER JOINT
flexion 90°
extension 0°
hyperextension 45°
abduction 90°
adduction 0°
outward rotation 90°
inward rotation 90°
horizontal flexion 90°
horizontal abduction 90°

NECK — cervical region
flexion 90°
extension 0°
hyperextension 45°
lateral flexion 45°
rotation 180° (total)

WRIST
flexion 80°-90°
extension 0°
hyperextention 80°-90°
ulnar flexion 35°-45°
radial flexion 20°-25°

METACARPAL-PHALANGEAL JT
flexion 90°
extension 0°
hyperextension 0°-20°
abduction 30°
adduction 0°

DISTAL INTERPHALANGEAL JT.
flexion 80°-90°
extension 0°

PROXIMAL INTERPHALANGEAL JT.
flexion 100°-110°
extension 0°

METATARSAL-PHALANGEAL JT.
flexion 20°
extension 0°
hyperextension 80°
abduction 15°-20°
adduction 0°

KNEE
flexion 130°-135°
extension 0°

PROXIMAL INTERPHALANGEAL JT
flexion 40°
extension 0°

ANKLE
plantar flexion 50°-60°
dorsi flexion 10°-20°

FOOT
plantar flexion 50°-60°
dorsi flexion 10°-20°
inversion 40°-45°
eversion 20°-25°
abduction 20°
adduction 45°
supination 45°
pronation 20°

DISTAL INTERPHALANGEAL JT.
flexion 50°
extension 0°

Figure 1: Range of Motion for Fundamental Movements: Anterior View

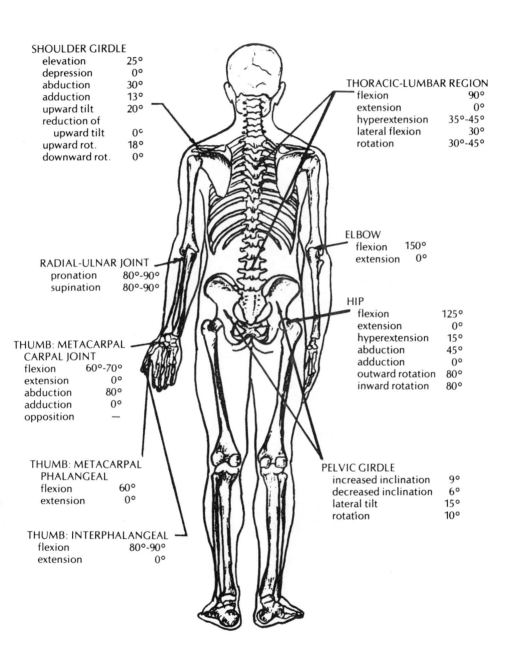

SHOULDER GIRDLE
elevation	25°
depression	0°
abduction	30°
adduction	13°
upward tilt	20°
reduction of	
upward tilt	0°
upward rot.	18°
downward rot.	0°

THORACIC-LUMBAR REGION
flexion	90°
extension	0°
hyperextension	35°-45°
lateral flexion	30°
rotation	30°-45°

ELBOW
flexion	150°
extension	0°

RADIAL-ULNAR JOINT
pronation	80°-90°
supination	80°-90°

HIP
flexion	125°
extension	0°
hyperextension	15°
abduction	45°
adduction	0°
outward rotation	80°
inward rotation	80°

THUMB: METACARPAL
CARPAL JOINT
flexion	60°-70°
extension	0°
abduction	80°
adduction	0°
opposition	—

THUMB: METACARPAL
PHALANGEAL
flexion	60°
extension	0°

PELVIC GIRDLE
increased inclination	9°
decreased inclination	6°
lateral tilt	15°
rotation	10°

THUMB: INTERPHALANGEAL
flexion	80°-90°
extension	0°

**Figure 2: Range of Motion for Fundamental Movements:
Posterior View**

The pinch test.

BODY COMPOSITION

There are no practical, relatively accurate nonlaboratory methods for measuring body composition. A simple test you can use to estimate your level of body fat is the "pinch test." The pinch test involves pinching your skin at certain points on your body. Since body fat tends to be deposited in certain areas of the body (as opposed to being evenly distributed), the pinch test will give a rough indication of the amount of fat you've collected in a given body area. To administer the pinch test, pinch your skin using your thumb and index finger. If the amount of skin between your fingers is greater than one inch, then you have an *excessive* amount of fat deposited in that area. One-half to one inch is considered to be too much, but still *moderate;* while less than one-half inch of fat is judged to be an *acceptable* amount of fat. The five areas of the body usually measured are the backs of the arms, the abdominal area surrounding the belly button, the trunk area (sides of your waist), the insides of the upper thighs, and the area right below the rib cage.

FITNESS EVALUATION

Now that you've tested your physical fitness components, you are ready to develop your personal fitness evaluation. I've made up a sample evaluation for you to follow, using the fictitious "Larry Martin" as a guide. You can substitute your test results for his and determine how fit you are and where improvement is needed.

In looking over the sample evaluation, you can see that, in general, Larry Martin is in good shape, although there's room for improvement in some areas. A regular program of Power-Walking will increase his level of cardiovascular fitness. His goal should be to achieve a Physical Efficiency Index (PEI)

SAMPLE FITNESS EVALUATION

Name: Larry Martin
Age: 24 years
Height: 6 feet
Weight: 175 pounds
Health: Excellent

Fitness Component	Test Measure	Test Score	Rating
Cardiovascular fitness	Post-step test heart rate (PEI)	78	Average
Muscular fitness	Chin-ups	10	Good
	Sit-ups	34	Poor
	Push-ups	50	Excellent
Flexibility	Trunk flexion	+3"	Above-average
Body composition	Pinch test:		
	trunk area	½"	Acceptable
	abdominal area	1½"	Unacceptable
	back of arms	½"	Acceptable

score of at least 85 (excellent rating). He also needs to work on his abdominal area. Sit-ups, combined with PowerWalking, should develop his stomach muscles. Finally, he is a few pounds overweight and has developed a slight paunch. Sound dieting habits, in conjunction with a regular program of exercise, will help him to lose weight and stay in excellent physical shape.

ESTABLISH OBJECTIVES

Once you've evaluated your level of fitness for each component, the next step is to establish realistic goals for your PowerWalking program. Your program goals should be based on at least three factors: an accurate evaluation of your existing level of fitness, a reasonable expectation of how much improvement in your fitness can be achieved considering the time and exercise conditions available, and a realistic assessment of how physically fit you really want and need to be, given your interests. Your answers to these questions will greatly affect the way you structure your PowerWalking program. Sample programs for beginning and advanced PowerWalking are outlined in Chapters 4 and 9.

CHART YOUR PROGRESS

For the duration of any conditioning program designed to improve fitness—particularly PowerWalking—you should chart and periodically evaluate your progress. This will enable you to determine whether your program is in fact effective. I strongly recommend that if you PowerWalk specifically for fitness improvement, you maintain a daily diary. In it you should note general comments about how you felt during the walk, the distance covered or amount of time spent, your pace, your body weight (measured at approximately the same time every day), your resting pulse rate (taken approximately 15 minutes after getting up in the morning), the amount of additional weight you carried (for advanced PowerWalkers), and any other information such as injuries or ailments that might prove useful in developing a future PowerWalking program or in altering your existing one. For example, if your goal is to be able to PowerWalk 2 miles in less than 24 minutes and you've been unsuccessful in reaching that goal for several months, your daily diary might be able to tell you why. At the least, it could suggest possible adjustments you could make to improve your performance. The key is information. Adjustments in both your program and your goals should be made on the basis of factual data, not intuition. Charting your progress will allow you to channel your efforts and energies better.

SCORING YOUR STEP TEST

TABLE 1. Fitness Scores for Men Based on Post-Exercise Pulse Count

Post-Exercise Pulse Count

												Fitness Score	
45	33	33	33	33	33	32	32	32	32	32	32	32	32
44	34	34	34	34	33	33	33	33	33	33	33	33	33
43	35	35	35	34	34	34	34	34	34	34	34	34	34
42	36	35	35	35	35	35	35	35	35	35	35	34	34
41	36	36	36	36	36	36	36	36	36	36	36	35	35
40	37	37	37	37	37	37	37	37	36	36	36	36	36
39	38	38	38	38	38	38	38	38	38	38	38	37	37
38	39	39	39	39	39	39	39	39	39	39	39	38	38
37	41	40	40	40	40	40	40	40	40	40	40	39	39
36	42	42	41	41	41	41	41	41	41	41	41	40	40
35	43	43	42	42	42	42	42	42	42	42	42	42	41
34	44	44	43	43	43	43	43	43	43	43	43	43	43
33	46	45	45	45	45	45	44	44	44	44	44	44	44
32	47	47	46	46	46	46	46	46	46	46	46	46	46
31	48	48	48	47	47	47	47	47	47	47	47	47	47
30	50	49	49	49	48	48	48	48	48	48	48	48	48
29	52	51	51	51	50	50	50	50	50	50	50	50	50
28	53	53	53	53	52	52	52	52	52	52	51	51	51
27	55	55	55	54	54	54	54	54	54	53	53	53	52
26	57	57	56	56	56	56	56	56	56	55	55	54	54
25	59	59	58	58	58	58	58	58	58	56	56	55	55
24	60	60	60	60	60	60	60	59	59	58	58	57	
23	62	62	61	61	61	61	61	60	60	60	59		
22	64	64	63	63	63	63	62	62	61	61			
21	66	66	65	65	65	64	64	64	62				
20	68	68	67	67	67	66	66	65					
Body weight	120	130	140	150	160	170	180	190	200	210	220	230	240

TABLE 2. Fitness Scores for Women
Based on Post-Exercise Pulse Count

Fitness Score

Post-Exercise Pulse Count	80	90	100	110	120	130	140	150	160	170	180	190
45										29	29	29
44								30	30	30	30	30
43							31	31	31	31	31	31
42			32	32	32	32	32	32	32	32	32	32
41			33	33	33	33	33	33	33	33	33	33
40			34	34	34	34	34	34	34	34	34	34
39			35	35	35	35	35	35	35	35	35	35
38			36	36	36	36	36	36	36	36	36	36
37			37	37	37	37	37	37	37	37	37	37
36		37	38	38	38	38	38	38	38	38	38	38
35	38	38	39	39	39	39	39	39	39	39	39	39
34	39	39	40	40	40	40	40	40	40	40	40	40
33	40	40	41	41	41	41	41	41	41	41	41	41
32	41	41	42	42	42	42	42	42	42	42	42	42
31	42	42	43	43	43	43	43	43	43	43	43	43
30	43	43	44	44	44	44	44	44	44	44	44	44
29	44	44	45	45	45	45	45	45	45	45	45	45
28	45	45	46	46	46	47	47	47	47	47	47	47
27	46	46	47	48	48	49	49	49	49	49		
26	47	48	49	50	50	51	51	51	51			
25	49	50	51	52	52	53	53					
24	51	52	53	54	54	55						
23	53	54	55	56	56	57						
Body weight	80	90	100	110	120	130	140	150	160	170	180	190

TABLE 3. Adjusting Fitness Scores of 30 to 50 for Age

Age-Adjusted Score

Enter Fitness Score →

Nearest Age	30	31	32	33	34	35	36	37	38	39	40	41	42	43	44	45	46	47	48	49	50
15	32	33	34	35	36	37	38	39	40	41	42	43	44	45	46	47	48	49	50	51	53
20	31	32	33	34	35	36	37	38	39	40	41	42	43	44	45	46	47	48	49	50	51
25	30	31	32	33	34	35	36	37	38	39	40	41	42	43	44	45	46	47	48	49	50
30	29	30	31	32	33	34	35	36	37	38	39	40	41	42	43	44	45	46	47	48	49
35	28	29	30	31	32	33	34	35	36	37	38	39	40	41	42	43	44	45	46	47	48
40	26	27	28	29	30	31	32	33	34	35	36	37	38	39	40	41	42	43	44	45	**47**
45	25	26	27	28	29	30	31	32	33	34	35	36	37	38	39	40	41	42	43	44	46
50	24	25	26	27	28	29	30	31	32	33	34	35	36	37	38	39	40	41	42	43	45
55	23	24	25	26	27	28	29	30	31	32	33	34	35	36	37	38	39	40	41	42	43
60	22	23	24	25	26	27	28	29	30	31	32	33	34	35	36	37	38	39	40	41	42
65	21	22	23	24	25	26	27	28	29	30	31	32	33	34	35	36	37	38	38	39	40

Adjusting Score for Age

Example: If your age is 40 years and you score 50 on the step test, your age-adjusted score is 47.

TABLE 4. Adjusting Fitness Scores of 51 to 72 for Age

Age-Adjusted Score

Enter Fitness Score →

Nearest Age	51	52	53	54	55	56	57	58	59	60	61	62	63	64	65	66	67	68	69	70	71	72
15	54	55	56	57	58	59	60	61	62	63	64	65	66	67	68	69	70	71	72	74	75	76
20	52	53	54	55	56	57	58	59	60	61	62	63	64	65	66	67	68	69	70	71	72	73
25	51	52	53	54	55	56	57	58	59	60	61	62	63	64	65	66	67	68	69	70	71	72
30	50	51	52	53	54	55	56	57	58	59	60	61	62	63	64	65	66	67	68	69	70	71
35	49	50	51	52	53	54	55	56	57	58	59	60	60	61	62	63	64	65	66	67	68	69
40	48	49	50	51	52	53	54	55	55	56	57	58	59	60	61	62	63	64	65	66	67	68
45	47	48	49	50	51	52	52	53	54	55	56	57	58	59	60	61	62	63	64	65	65	66
50	45	46	47	48	49	50	51	52	53	53	54	55	56	57	58	58	59	61	61	62	63	64
55	44	45	46	46	47	48	49	50	51	52	53	53	54	55	56	57	58	59	59	60	61	62
60	42	43	44	45	46	46	47	48	49	50	51	51	52	53	54	55	56	57	57	58	59	60
65	41	42	42	43	44	45	46	46	47	48	49	50	50	51	52	53	54	54	55	56	57	58

Adjusting Score for Age

Example: If your age is 40 years and you score 60 on the step test, your age-adjusted score is 56.

TABLE 5. Physical Fitness Ratings Based on Age-Adjusted Scores

PHYSICAL FITNESS RATING—MEN
(Use Age-Adjusted Score)

Nearest Age	Superior	Excellent	Very Good	Good	Fair	Poor	Very Poor
15	57+	56–52	51–47	46–42	41–37	36–32	31–
20	56+	55–51	50–46	45–41	40–36	35–31	30–
25	55+	54–50	49–45	44–40	39–35	34–30	29–
30	54+	53–49	48–44	43–39	38–34	33–29	28–
35	53+	52–48	47–43	42–38	37–33	32–28	27–
40	52+	51–47	46–42	41–37	36–32	31–27	26–
45	51+	50–46	45–41	40–36	35–31	30–26	25–
50	50+	49–45	44–40	39–35	34–30	29–25	24–
55	49+	48–44	43–39	38–34	33–29	28–24	23–
60	48+	47–43	42–38	37–33	32–28	27–23	22–
65	47+	46–42	41–37	36–32	31–27	26–22	21–

PHYSICAL FITNESS RATING—WOMEN
(Use Age-Adjusted Score)

Nearest Age	Superior	Excellent	Very Good	Good	Fair	Poor	Very Poor
15	54+	53–49	48–44	43–39	38–34	33–29	28–
20	53+	52–48	47–43	42–38	37–33	32–28	27–
25	52+	51–47	46–42	41–37	36–32	31–27	26–
30	51+	50–46	45–41	40–36	35–31	30–26	25–
35	50+	49–45	44–40	39–35	34–30	29–25	24–
40	49+	48–44	43–39	38–34	33–29	28–24	23–
45	48+	47–43	42–38	37–33	32–28	27–23	22–
50	47+	46–42	41–37	36–32	31–27	26–22	21–
55	46+	45–41	40–36	35–31	30–26	25–21	20–
60	45+	44–40	39–35	34–30	29–25	24–20	19–
65	44+	43–39	38–34	33–29	28–24	23–20	19–

7

Winning the Losing Game

 espite the fact that I have been an ardent practitioner of physical fitness since I was a teenager, there have been times in my life when I have been faced with the necessity of "winning the losing battle." During my days as a movie actor, I frequently had to assume different body proportions from one role to the next. When I played the title role in *Hercules*, for instance, the movie's producer wanted me to weigh a muscular 210 pounds. For the role of a cowboy in the movie *A Long Ride from Hell*, I was required to reduce my weight to 190 pounds in order to fit the director's concept of how a cowboy should look. I soon discovered that the only way to lose those pounds was to combine an exercise program with a sound diet.

The value of this approach was re-emphasized to me two years ago when I had a shoulder operation. I was laid up for

almost six weeks afterward, during which time I gained a few unwanted pounds. Fortunately, I soon was able to resume PowerWalking. By watching my diet closely and exercising regularly, I was able to lose weight. This approach will also work for you. You don't need magic pills, newly discovered diets from the geographical social centers of the United States, or Spartan eating habits to control your weight. What will work for you is what worked for me: a program based on equal parts of exercise, proper nutrition, and common sense.

Controlling your body weight begins and ends with food and drink. When you eat too much, you gain weight. When you eat less than you need, you lose weight. And if you eat within the limits of your needs once your weight is normal, your weight will remain fairly stable.

There is absolutely nothing magical or mystical about winning the battle to lose weight. The key is a rigid adherence to one approach—COMMON SENSE. Basically all weight change can be viewed as the end result of a weight-control continuum, as shown here:

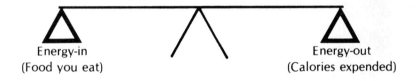

Energy-in
(Food you eat)

Energy-out
(Calories expended)

If the level of food you eat (energy-in) *exceeds* your expenditure of calories (energy-out), you'll gain weight. If the amount of food you eat is *less* than your energy expenditure, you'll lose weight. If you want to control your weight, all you have to do is develop an understanding of the factors that affect each end of the continuum and then adopt a "common sense" approach to achieving your personal objectives.

Most physicians recommend that the maximum amount of weight to lose in any given week without strict medical supervision is 2 pounds. Since there are approximately 3500 calories in a pound of body weight, this means that if you want to lose 2 pounds in a week, you'll have to achieve a negative energy balance of 7000 calories (3500 × 2 pounds). In other words, the amount of energy you expend during the week has to be 7000 calories greater than the amount of food you eat.

In theory, maintaining a negative energy balance (more "out" than "in") is a relatively simple task. Obviously, it's important to know how many calories are in the foods you eat and how many calories are expended by the activities you typically do. The table that follows lists the approximate caloric values of selected foods. On the other end of the scale, a second table presents the amount of energy expended by selected activities.

As you can see by the energy expenditure table, the number of calories you burn up in a given activity ranges from 80 per hour for sleeping to approximately 900 per hour for activities in which most of your body's musculature is involved (for example, jogging, swimming, and PowerWalking). In general, the more muscles involved, the greater the energy expenditure. As the figures indicate, no activity will allow you to use more calories than PowerWalking. As an added bonus, no activity is better than PowerWalking for developing total fitness in the safest, quickest way.

"Winning the losing game" involves more than merely being aware of the calorie-energy continuum, however. In order to lose weight safely and keep it off permanently, you must do at least two things: eat a nutritionally balanced diet and retrain your eating habits. Above all, your efforts must be guided by COMMON SENSE.

Caloric Values of Selected Foods

Food	Weight or Approximate Measure	Calories
Milk Group		
Cheese, cheddar	1⅛ cube	115
Cheese, cottage, creamed	¼ cup	65
Cream, coffee	1 tbsp	30
Milk, fluid, skim		
(buttermilk)	1 cup	90
Milk, fluid, whole	1 cup	160
Meat Group		
Beans, dry, canned	¾ cup	233
Beef, pot roast	3 oz	245
Chicken	½ breast-with bone	155
Egg	1 medium	80
Frankfurter	1 medium	170
Haddock	1 fillet	140
Ham, boiled	2 oz	135
Liver, beef	2 oz	130
Peanut butter	2 tbsp	190
Pork chop	1 chop	260
Salmon, canned	½ cup	120
Sausage bologna	2 slices	173
Vegetable Group		
Beans, snap, green	½ cup	15
Broccoli	½ cup	20
Cabbage, shredded, raw	½ cup	10
Carrots, diced	½ cup	23
Corn, canned	½ cup	85
Lettuce leaves	2 large or 4 small	10
Peas, green	½ cup	58
Potato, white	1 medium	90
Spinach	½ cup	20
Squash, winter	½ cup	65
Sweet potato	1 medium	155
Tomato juice, canned	½ cup (small glass)	23

Food	Weight or Approximate Measure	Calories
Fruit Group		
Apple, raw	1 medium	70
Apricots, dried/stewed	½ cup	135
Banana, raw	1 medium	100
Cantaloupe	½ melon	60
Grapefruit	½ medium	45
Orange	1 medium	65
Orange juice, fresh	½ cup (small glass)	55
Peaches, canned	½ cup with syrup	100
Pineapple juice, canned	½ cup (small glass)	68
Prunes, dried, cooked	5 with juice	160
Strawberries, raw	½ cup, capped	30
Bread-Cereal Group		
Bread, white, enriched	1 slice	70
Cornflakes, fortified	1⅓ cup	133
Macaroni, enriched, cooked	¾ cup	115
Oatmeal, cooked	⅔ cup	87
Rice, cooked	¾ cup	140
Fats Group		
Bacon, crisp	2 slices	90
Butter or fortified margarine	1 tbsp	100
Oils, salad or cooking	1 tbsp	125
Sweets Group		
Beverages, cola type	6 oz	75
Sugar, granulated	1 tbsp	40

Energy Expended by a 150-Pound Person, Various Activities

Activity	Gross Energy Cost—CAL. PER HR.
Rest and Light Activity	**80–200**
Lying down or sleeping	80
Sitting	100
Driving an automobile	120
Standing	140
Moderate Activity	**200–350**
Bicycling (5½ mph)	210
Walking (2½ mph)	210
Canoeing (2½ mph)	230
Golf	250
Bowling	270
Fencing	300
Rowboating (2½ mph)	300
Swimming (¼ mph)	300
Walking (3¾ mph)	300
Badminton	350
Horseback riding (trotting)	350
Volleyball	350
Roller skating	350
Vigorous Activity	**over 350**
Table tennis	360
Ice skating (10 mph)	400
Wood chopping	400
Tennis	420
Water skiing	480
Hill climbing (100 ft. per hr.)	490
Skiing (10 mph)	600
Squash and handball	600
Cycling (13 mph)	660
Scull rowing (race)	840
Swimming (2 mph)	900
Running (10 mph)	900
PowerWalking (5 mph)	900

NUTRITIONALLY SOUND DIET

In addition to calories, every food contains nutrients—six groupings of body-building ingredients that are absolutely essential for life. It is important to remember that no one food contains all the nutrients your body requires. Since every nutrient has a specific use in your body, a combination of nutrients is needed for a well-balanced diet. If you eat a nutritionally poor diet, sooner or later you will become ill. In fact, a nutritionally unsound diet could eventually result in death. The actual nutritional needs of individuals vary from person to person. What follows is a list of the six basic nutrients and a brief description of the functions of each.

Protein. Proteins are the fundamental structural element of every cell of the body. Its name is derived from a Greek word meaning of first importance. Proteins are composed of carbon hydrogen, oxygen, nitrogen and sulfur. Protein is necessary to build and repair body tissue but some proteins are better than others for these purposes. A complete protein contains the essential amino acids in the most useful proportions and will best build and repair tissue. The best proportioned proteins are found in such foods as meat, fish, cheese, eggs, poultry, and milk. Plant proteins are not as complete—these are found in grains, legumes (such as beans, peas) and nuts and need balancing with animal proteins to supply the body with usable protein elements.

Carbohydrate. Carbohydrate foods are the major sources of calories for people all over the world. They make up 50 to 60 percent of the American diet and in other countries the percentage is even higher. They are easily digested and constitute the cheapest form of food energy. They are composed of carbon, hydrogen, and oxygen and exist as complex sugars and starches which are converted, through digestion, to simpler sugars which the body can utilize for energy. Carbohydrates include cellulose, which is important as roughage in the digestive tract. All carbohydrate eventually becomes glucose, a simple sugar which travels through the bloodstream and serves as a source of energy for the body tissues. Important carbohydrates are sugars, starches, syrups, and honey and are major constituents of vegetables, fruits, breads, and cereals.

Fats. Fats are compounds of fatty acids and glycerol — another complex structure of carbon, hydrogen and oxygen — insoluble in water and greasy to the touch. The different fats in each food help give the food its particular flavor and texture. Fats are especially important because they produce more concentrated energy, almost 2½ times as much as either proteins or carbohydrates. They have a high satiety value — because they take longer to digest than other nutrients they keep us from feeling hungry for longer periods of time. Fats also are carriers of the fat soluble vitamins — A, D, E, and K. They can be generally classified as animal fats and vegetable fats — the former found in meats, eggs, milk, butter — the latter in margarine, vegetable oils, mayonnaise, and salad dressing.

Minerals. Minerals are found in foods mixed or combined with proteins, fats, and carbohydrates. Calcium and phosphorus are minerals which give rigidity to the bones and teeth. Milk is a good source of both. Minerals are also needed for normal blood clotting and proper functioning of the nervous system. Iron is a mineral essential in the diet since lack of it can produce anemia and make us feel tired and listless. Meat and enriched bread are good sources of iron. Other minerals are essential to help maintain a normal acid-base balance in the body and other important functions.

Vitamins. Vitamins are complex organic compounds which are found in foodstuffs. They perform specific vital functions in the cells and tissues of the body. They are called accessory food factors and are needed for normal health which includes good eyesight, strong teeth and bones, freedom from infection and disease, normal functioning of the nervous system, tissue respiration, and other functions.

Water. Water is also essential to life. It is a necessary constituent of digestive juices and of every cell and tissue of the body. Two thirds of the body weight is water. It is a major component of blood, lymph and other secretions of the body, and helps regulate body temperature. As a carrier, it aids digestion, absorption, circulation, and excretion. Moisture is necessary for the functioning of every organ of the body. Most foods contain a large percentage of water.

Given the importance of nutrients, it is obviously important to choose wisely what you eat. Because you might sacrifice or compromise your nutritional needs, it would be foolish to cut out foods from your diet merely for the sake of cutting down on your calories. If you're to win the losing game safely and for any reasonable length of time, you must eat a sound (although reduced) diet. The obvious question then is, How can you be sure that you're eating a balanced diet? Although there are several steps you could take to ensure that you're eating properly, one of the simplest and most practical is to eat foods each day selected from the four basic food groups:

Milk Group (includes milk, ice cream, cheese, yogurt). Most of the body's calcium comes from milk and milk products. Calcium builds bones and teeth and helps the muscles, heart, and nerves function properly. Foods in this group also provide the body with significant amounts of protein, riboflavin (vitamin B$_2$), vitamin A, and other important nutrients.

Meat Group (includes meat, poultry, fish, eggs). This group provides the body with protein, which is essential for strength and for maintaining and repairing body tissue. Young people need protein to grow. It also helps form the red blood cells and antibodies you need to fight infection. Foods in this group also provide the body with iron, thiamine (vitamin B), riboflavin (vitamin B$_2$), and niacin. Among other sources of protein are peanut butter, lima beans, and soybeans.

Vegetable-Fruit Group. Dark green and yellow vegetables and apples, pears, and bananas provide vitamin A. Citrus fruits, strawberries, cantaloupe, tomatoes, cabbage, potatoes, green peppers, and broccoli provide vitamin C.

Bread and Cereal Group. Foods in this group, especially those made from enriched or restored whole grain, provide the body with a large amount of iron, niacin, the B vitamins, and carbohydrates. Carbohydrates consist of starches and sugars, a major source of energy and cellulose that provides your diet with necessary bulk.

Recommended daily servings from the four basic food groups are two servings each from the milk group and from the meat and protein-rich foods group, and four servings each from the cereal group and the fruit and vegetable group. These servings will of themselves supply essentially all necessary nutrients, no matter how large you are or how active your exercise.

RETRAINING YOUR EATING HABITS

Your eating habits are a major factor in your being overweight. In many instances, your habits dictate when and how you eat, what you eat, and how much you eat.

Take, for example, the habit of eating quickly. Your body's mechanism for letting you know when you've had enough to eat is based on your blood-sugar level. The intake of food prompts a relatively slow response on this level. When you eat rapidly, you often eat more food than you normally would before the satiety mechanism has a chance to work. Another example is the practice of eating your meals in front of the television set and developing the habit of eating something *every* time you watch television, regardless of whether or not it's meal time. And if you're a person who has a cup of coffee and a dessert every time a neighbor drops in for a chat, you've developed a bad habit as far as weight control is concerned.

The key is to eat three normal meals a day and, if at all possible, avoid snacking between meals. Change your living patterns that contribute to snacking and other bad eating habits. Keep a record of what you eat and when you eat it. Many people snack unconsciously. Every time you eat something, you're making a deposit in your body's energy bank. Too many deposits and you'll gain unwanted weight. Remember the age-old dictum "once on the lips, forever on the hips."

HOW MUCH SHOULD YOU WEIGH?

There is no simple method for determining how much you should weigh. Standard lists of desirable weight levels (such as the list on p 113) are based on height-weight ratios If this guideline is acceptable to you, I encourage you to use it. Yet these tables have a major limitation. Your primary concern should not be how much you weigh but how much of your body is fat (adipose tissue), as opposed to lean muscle mass, bones, organs, and so on. Body fat is your energy. With only a few exceptions, it contributes *nothing* to your well-being. Lean muscle mass, on the other hand, is a positive force for your health and well-being. The problem with the recommended weight tables is that they do not tell you whether you have too much or too little fat. For men, a body-fat level of 19 percent is considered obese, with a level of 10 percent or less as the target goal. Since women have more adipose tissue than men, 26 percent body fat is considered obese, and 19 percent or less is the recommended level.

Desirable Weight Levels for Adult Men and Women
(Based on Metropolitan Life Insurance Company tables)

Desirable Weight/Men

Height	Small Frame	Medium Frame	Large Frame
5ft. 1in.	113	121	131
5ft. 2in.	116	124	134
5ft. 3in.	119	127	137
5ft. 4in.	122	130	140
5ft. 5in.	126	134	144
5ft. 6in.	130	138	149
5ft. 7in.	134	142	154
5ft. 8in.	138	146	158
5ft. 9in.	142	150	162
5ft. 10in.	146	155	166
5ft. 11in.	150	159	171
6ft. 0	154	164	176
6ft. 1in.	159	168	181
6ft. 2in.	163	173	186
6ft. 3in.	167	178	191

Desirable Weight/Women

Height	Small Frame	Medium Frame	Large Frame
4ft. 8in.	94	101	111
4ft. 9in.	97	103	113
4ft. 10in.	99	106	116
4ft. 11in.	102	109	119
5ft. 0	105	112	122
5ft. 1in.	108	115	125
5ft. 2in.	111	119	129
5ft. 3in.	114	123	133
5ft. 4in.	118	127	137
5ft. 5in.	122	131	141
5ft. 6in.	126	135	145
5ft. 7in.	130	139	149
5ft. 8in.	134	143	153
5ft. 9in.	138	147	158
5ft. 10in.	142	151	162

You could, for example, fall within the range of your recommended weight as listed on the height-weight table and still
have an unacceptably high level of body fat. By the same token, you could weigh more than the table recommends and
still have a below-average percentage of fat if you have more
muscle mass than the "average" person. The point is, don't be
misled by the frequently arbitrary tools and techniques for determining how much you should weigh. When in doubt, you
should use both the pinch test and the "eyeball exam." Since
fat tends to accumulate in certain areas of your body (back of
your arms, sides of your hips, your belly-button region, bottom
of your pectoral-chest-muscles, inside of your thighs), you can
readily tell if too much fat has accumulated in a given region.
Pinch the area. If you can pinch more than 1 inch in thickness
between your fingers, there is an above-average chance that
you're carrying too much fat.

The last test is the eyeball exam. Stand in front of a mirror in
your underwear. Unless you have a trick circus mirror, your
eyes will tell you the truth—the whole, sometimes painful,
truth.

DIETING HINTS

No "master diet" fits all individuals, but there are general
guidelines that can assist you if you are interested in losing
weight:

- Decrease caloric intake. If you stop eating an extra 25
  calories or so a day, you may stop gaining weight. And
  if you cut back 100 calories less than you need a day,
  you will lose 10 to 12 pounds a year.
- Eat your largest meal at lunch time.
- Learn to eat slowly and chew thoroughly.
- Limit portions of food at meals to one average serving.

- Never take second helpings.
- Omit or drastically restrict free fats—butter, margarine, mayonnaise, salad oils, cooking fats. Sufficient fat is present in lean meats, fish, poultry, eggs, and cheese to ensure adequate use of the fat-soluble vitamins A, D, E, and K.
- Omit or drastically restrict free sweets—jelly, jam, honey, syrups, sugar, candy, pies, pastries, and most other desserts.
- Restrict or eliminate intake of alcoholic beverages.
- Eat a good breakfast and never skip a meal.
- Never use food as a reward.
- Learn to practice moderation. If you decide to indulge in a high-calorie food, you should eat it slowly and eat one half or less than you normally would.
- Buy a good scale and use it. Weigh yourself once a week and keep a written record of your body weight.
- Keep a food diary. Record in detail all that you eat and drink for a week. This helps stiffen resistance to dietary temptations. It is also helpful in revealing possible unconscious slips in your dieting.

MYTHS ABOUT DIETING

EXERCISE INCREASES YOUR APPETITE

If you are doing more physically, will your appetite necessarily increase? The antithesis of this would mean that if you did very little, you wouldn't be as hungry. Personally, I'm hungrier when I do nothing, or practically nothing. When I'm active, my appetite lessens. According to many authorities, intense exercise for even relatively short periods, such as 15 minutes of PowerWalking, decreases your appetite. Your desire for food is decreased due to the decrease in blood flow to the stomach. Even after vigorous exercise, the appetite rarely increases above normal. Think about it—after an active game or workout, can you eat a big meal?

SPOT REDUCING

Spot reducing is a cruel hoax people play on themselves. How many of you have said, "If I could only take a knife and cut four inches from my stomach and hips!" Some comments I hear frequently from friends of my wife are, "How do I get rid of my stomach?" "How do I get rid of my rear end?" "I don't need to lose weight or inches anywhere else, just in certain spots. I want exercises for those areas only." *There is no such thing as spot reduction.* The only thing you can do is to tone up muscles everywhere through proper diet and exercise. The loss of fat tends to be uniform all over the body in proportion to the amount present in any given spot. Vigorous exercise, such as PowerWalking, combined with a sensible diet, provides the best means of reducing your level of body fat. Don't focus on any particular fatty area you've cultivated over the years. The weight will come off slowly from all over your body. Unfortunately, a weight loss will not restrict itself initially to the largest accumulation of fat.

RUBBER SWEATSUITS AND SAUNAS

Many people try to "win the losing game" by wearing a rubber sweatsuit and sweating off a few pounds. This is a useless, and sometimes a dangerous, approach. If you wear a rubber suit while exercising, I guarantee you that you will lose a few pounds of water. But by the same token, I guarantee that as soon as you drink fluids, the water—and weight—you lost will be replaced. Rubberized suits also can be dangerous. When you wear a rubber sweatsuit, your internal body temperature rises to a very high level because the sweat trapped by the suit is unable to evaporate and "cool" your blood. When your body's heat is raised beyond its normal range, a tremendous burden is placed on its heat regulating mechanisms. In some cases, the high temperature can cause severe problems. Taking it to extremes, a heat stroke, and in some cases death, can result.

You can use the same argument against the value of sitting in a sauna for weight reduction. The only weight lost is water—water that is quickly replaced when you consume fluids. In fact, sitting in a sauna (or steam room) for an extended period of time can cause heat-related medical problems similar to those resulting from wearing a rubber sweatsuit.

POSTURE

One thing that will help you "win the losing game" without sacrificing a bite of your favorite snack or a sip of your favorite beverage is maintaining proper posture. People could look 100 percent better if they had better posture. Many people slouch; they put their weight to the side of the hips, automatically causing the stomach to protrude. If you stand erect, your abdomen is flatter and your overall appearance improves due to proper body alignment.

There are some specific exercises you can do to improve your posture. Stand with your back to a wall, feet about 18 inches apart, knees bent. Flatten the small of your back against the wall by tilting your pelvis foward. Your hand should not be able to slide between your back and the wall. Hold. Then relax. At first you might find this a difficult exercise to do. Gradually stand against the wall without bending your knees so much.

**Proper body
alignment improves
overall appearance.**

Or you can try an exercise that is more for the beginner. Lie on the floor with your knees bent and your feet flat. Hold in your stomach and try to push the small of your back flat to the floor. Hold for a few seconds. Relax and repeat.

PowerWalking also can have a positive effect on your posture. Because you have to maintain correct body alignment (including posture) while you're doing the PowerWalk, you become more aware of your posture. Poor posture is frequently the by-product of forgetting to stand up straight. Make good posture a habit. Stand tall and you'll look more fit. PowerWalking can affect your posture in another way. Since it tones your muscles, your ability to physically maintain the proper posture is improved.

THE KEYS TO SUCCESS

The keys to "winning the losing game" are common sense and motivation. No magic pills or magic diets will produce the weight loss you are seeking. There is no magic route to follow. If you're overweight, it's because you ate more calories than you expended as energy. The only way you can lose weight is to change your eating habits and control what you eat.

As for motivation, the moment you started to read this chapter, you took the first step toward losing weight. By your interest, you are admitting to yourself that you want to rid yourself of those "extra" pounds. This is a critical factor. You must make a firm commitment to losing weight if you want to "win the losing game." The tools and techniques that are necessary for you to be a winner have been presented in this chapter. PowerWalking can help. But only you can make the commitment. And remember, "the pounds you lose will be yours."

Mobile
Meditation

None of us is immune to pressures—job and financial worries, family concerns, illnesses, large and small emergencies. These pressures manifest themselves in us in numerous forms including tension, anger, frustration, worry, and fear. Collectively, these emotions frequently cause considerable wear and tear on both our physical and mental well-being. Anything that can help relieve these pressures is a blessing. Over the years, I have found that PowerWalking has the power to relieve stress. Time and again, PowerWalking has provided me with a strong sense of both emotional and physical relief. This results primarily from a process I call MOBILE MEDITATION.

Meditation can be defined as an exercise in contemplation. The nature and focus of the contemplation can vary from individual to individual. Some people try to make their minds go

**Mobile meditation
clears the mind
and stimulates
creative thinking.**

blank initially and then concentrate on something very simple such as their breathing patterns, the sky, the environment around them, and so on. Other people try to focus initially on a few pleasant things and then think about subjects of more substantive nature. Regardless of the approach followed, the foundation of meditation is the same: MIND CONTROL. With practice, you'll find that you can direct and channel your thoughts to almost any given subject while PowerWalking.

WHY MEDITATE?

As Christmas Humphreys wrote in his book *Concentration and Meditation:* "[The purpose of meditation] is three fold: to dominate the lower, separate self, to develop the mind's own higher faculties toward a vision of life's essential unity, and to unite this dual process in one's continuous spiritual unfolding." Jim Lilliefors, in his book *Total Running: All About the Mental and Spiritual Side of Running,* put it another way: "The purpose of meditation . . . is subtle and all-encompassing so that you can have a clearer vision, more self-assurance, and a better understanding of your own psyche."

Although my personal explanation of the value of meditation probably isn't as ethereal as that of either Humphreys or Lilliefors, I am a firm believer in the positive effects of meditating while exercising. For me, mobile meditation accomplishes several things. It allows me to clear my mind. With a clearer mind, I find that my thinking is more rational. As a result, I'm able to solve problems more easily. I'm more productive because I can better focus on a problem and its solutions. It lets me concentrate on those aspects of my life I feel are important. For example, when PowerWalking in the morning, I'm often able to plan my activities for the entire day. Details and plans that would otherwise require notes or reminders become clear and easy to remember.

Meditation also stimulates my creative processes. New ideas flow like rainwater. Many times I'm bursting with ideas at the end of my PowerWalk. The minute I get home, I jot them down.

Perhaps the greatest value of mobile meditation is that it greatly relaxes me. It renews and refreshes me both physically and mentally. Scientists firmly believe that stress directly and indirectly kills thousands of people annually. People are too tense. They don't exercise enough. They worry too much. Instead of taking sound actions that will help them relieve the stress, they look for a "quick fix." How much better off, for example, would a person be who had the good sense to relax by substituting 15 minutes of mobile meditation for two martinis.

FEELING GOOD

One of the techniques I have found to be particularly successful while PowerWalking is to mentally say or chant a series of verse that I coordinate with my rhythmic breathing. For example, my rhythmic breathing pattern consists of three breaths in and then three breaths out. Each verse consists of two lines of three syllables per line. Each syllable is mentally said or chanted in concert with a specific breath.

For my own use, I've grouped the verses I like best into distinct categories. Here are my favorites:

Posture	*Calming*
Walk - ing - tall	Breath - ing - deep
Strid - ing - out	Feel - ing - calm

Pepper - Upper	*Losing Weight*
Ex - er - cise	Los - ing - weight
En - er - gize	Feel - ing - great

Fitness

Shap - ing - up	Trim - ming - down
Look - ing - good	Look - ing - good
Look - ing - good	Los - ing - weight
Feel - ing - fit	Gain - ing - health

REDUCING STRESS

Over the years, I have identified six steps that I combine with my PowerWalking program to help me relieve or prevent stress. These are the steps I take:

- *Balance work with play.* I schedule time for activities that I enjoy.
- *Get enough sleep and rest.* No one can sustain his or her health for long without sufficient sleep and rest. I always try to get plenty of sleep.
- *Work off tensions.* PowerWalking is a great way to accomplish this.
- *Don't take on too much.* I try to remember that there is a limit to everyone's capacity. As a general rule of thumb, I try never to do too much with the time and resources at my disposal.
- *Learn to accept what you cannot change.* I feel foolish when I get upset about circumstances that are truly beyond my control.
- *Look for the best in other people.* Humbling though it may be, it is a valuable trait to accept the fact that no one is faultless including yourself; more often than not, people are trying to do their best.

Unfortunately, people will aways face a certain amount of stress. How you manage that stress will go a long way toward determining the quality of your life and your level of well-being. For me, mobile meditation diffuses the negative effects of such pressures. It saddens me to see people who are literally being buried under the hustle and bustle of our technocratic society. PowerWalking offers them a convenient, safe way out of this dilemma. It's almost as if William Cullen Bryant was speaking directly to each of them almost a century ago when he said: "Go forth, under the open sky, and listen to nature's teaching." In his own way, Bryant was offering the perfect manifesto for PowerWalking.

Super Fitness

Once you've raised your fitness level to the point where you can PowerWalk on all kinds of terrain—flat and hilly—and sustain your pace at the proper rate, you have met the prerequisites to proceed to the final stage of PowerWalking—ADVANCED POWERWALKING. Advanced PowerWalking is a more intense form of Power-Walking. Its intensity is derived from manipulating the sixth component of PowerWalking—the amount of additional weight carried while exercising.

The value of increasing the intensity of PowerWalking by carrying additional weight came to me one day after a windstorm when I was on one of my walks. I saw two rather large avocados lying on the road; not wanting to see them go to waste, I picked them up. Since the outfit I was wearing didn't have any pockets, I carried one in each hand. I discovered that it felt invigorating to have the extra weight in my hands as I walked. The avocados probably weighed no more than half a pound each, but they seemed to help balance the arm swing. Shortly thereafter, I developed my own hand weights. Essentially they look like small dumbbells. The size and shape of the weights you use is entirely optional. Most sporting goods stores sell small dumbbells. You can also make your own. One simple idea is to fill a beanbag with lead shot to the weight you require, then sew up the bag.

If you would like information about ordering the PowerWalking weights I use in this book, write to:

Classic Image Enterprises
P.O. Box 807
Valley Center, California 92082

Some of my hand weights weigh 1¼ pounds (½ kilo), while I have others weighing 2½ pounds (1 kilo) and 5 pounds (2 kilos). Personally, I prefer walking with the 5 pounders. Naturally, when starting your advanced program, you should begin with 1¼-pound weights. After several weeks of training, you'll feel comfortable carrying the weights. At that point, you can increase the amount of weight carried in your hands. Most people graduate to 2½-pound and 5-pound weights within a few months.

Through an extensive period of trial and error, I discovered that I achieved maximum results from my advanced Power-Walking program by carrying up to 20 percent of my body weight while I walked. In the beginning, my major problem was figuring out where to carry the extra weight. I tried holding more than 5-pound weights in each hand, but found that I could not maintain the proper swinging motion of my arms while carrying the added weight. Not only did it affect my arm swing, but it also cut down the length of my stride. Obviously, that's the last thing I want to do, since a long stride is one of the most important components of PowerWalking. As a result, I

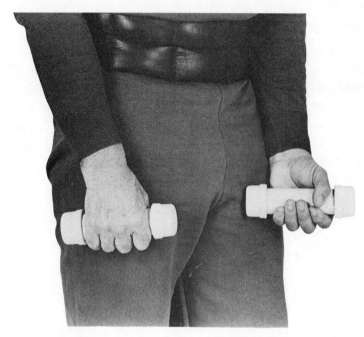

Weight belt and hand weights in place.

Ankle weights in place.
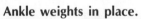

**Wearing all the weights
for advanced PowerWalking.**

now limit the amount of hand weights I carry to 5 pounds in each hand.

Ten pounds, however, constitutes 20 percent of the body weight of a person weighing only 50 pounds. Since you obviously weigh more than 50 pounds, the question of where you should carry the added weight arises. I solved the problem by wearing most of the additional weight around my waist. To accomplish this, I devised a belt that is weighted with shot. The shot can be added or removed to adjust the weight. Again by trial and error, I found that my program worked best when I wore approximately 20 pounds around my waist in addition to the hand-held weights. The ability of the waist to support the extra weight is illustrated by backpackers who carry 40- to 60-pound packs on their backs. Through the use of a wide waistband, most of the weight of the pack rests on their hips. Your waist is a natural place to carry extra weight.

The ankles are another ideal place for carrying additional weight while walking. I wear 2½-pound weights on each ankle. The extra weight I carry is distributed over three areas: hand-held weights, a weight belt, and ankle weights.

It is important to remember that at no time should you permit the extra weight you're carrying to compromise the proper mechanics of PowerWaiking. Your stride should remain at a maximum length. Your arm swing should be coordinated with the actions of your legs, and your breathing should be rhythmic and deep. If the amount or placement of the extra weight keeps you from PowerWalking properly, either reduce the amount of extra weight or change the location of the weight.

BREATHING VARIATIONS

The advanced PowerWalker can keep up his heart rate at the target level while walking downhill or can simulate the effect of walking on an uphill grade if there is none on the course by using this technique: *Inhale* for three steps (Left-Right-Left), *hold* for three steps (Right-Left-Right), then *exhale* for three steps (Left-Right-Left). An alternate method is to inhale for three, hold for six, and exhale for three (depending on your fitness level).

If you find that your cardio-pulmonary system is in such good shape that the inhaling for three, holding for six, and exhaling for three still doesn't maintain your heart rate at your target level, try inhaling for three steps, *holding for nine,* and exhaling for three; or, if necessary, inhale for three, *hold for twelve,* and exhale for three. One of these variations is bound to be right for your fitness level.

Finally, another breathing variation that has proven very effective in advanced PowerWalking to up the heart rate requires inhaling for three paces, holding for three, exhaling for three, and holding for three. The photographs on the following pages show the proper form for advanced PowerWalking.

When wearing the weights, it is important to maintain the proper form for PowerWalking.

Advanced PowerWalking in action.

ADVANCED POWERWALKING PROGRAMS

Here are twelve sample advanced PowerWalking programs. Select the program that fits your age group and adjust the program as needed through personal trial and error.

PROGRAM 1. Super Fitness PowerWalking for a 150-Pound Man 29 Years of Age or Younger

Week (3 times per week minimum)	Distance (in miles)	Time Allowed (recommended guidelines in minutes)	Extra Weight (H=hand weights W=waist belt A=ankle weights)		
1	½	6–10	H-1 lb.		
2	1	12–15	H-1 lb.		
3	1	12–14	H-1 lb.		
4	1	12–14	H-1 lb.	W-5 lb.	
5	1½	20–25	H-1 lb.	W-5 lb.	
6	1½	20–25	H-2 lb.	W-5 lb.	
7	1½	19–24	H-2 lb.	W-5 lb.	
8	1½	19–24	H-2 lb.	W-10 lb.	
9	1½	18–23	H-2 lb.	W-10 lb.	
10	1½	18–23	H-2 lb.	W-10 lb.	
11	2	25–32	H-2 lb.	W-12½ lb.	
12	2	25–32	H-3 lb.	W-12½ lb.	A-1 lb.
13	2	24–31	H-3 lb.	W-12½ lb.	A-1 lb.
14	2	24–31	H-3 lb.	W-15 lb.	A-1 lb.
15	2	24–30	H-3 lb.	W-15 lb.	A-1 lb.

PROGRAM 2. Super Fitness PowerWalking for a 175-Pound Man 29 Years of Age or Younger

Week (3 times per week minimum)	Distance (in miles)	Time Allowed (recommended guidelines in minutes)	Extra Weights (H=hand weights W=waist belt A=ankle weights)		
1	½	6–10	H-1 lb.		
2	1	12–15	H-1 lb.		
3	1	12–14	H-2 lb.		
4	1	12–14	H-2 lb.	W-5 lb.	
5	1½	20–25	H-3 lb.	W-5 lb.	
6	1½	20–25	H-3 lb.	W-5 lb.	
7	1½	19–24	H-3 lb.	W-5 lb.	
8	1½	19–24	H-3 lb.	W-10 lb.	
9	1½	18–23	H-4 lb.	W-10 lb.	
10	1½	18–23	H-4 lb.	W-15 lb.	
11	2	25–32	H-4 lb.	W-15 lb.	
12	2	25–32	H-4 lb.	W-15 lb.	A-1 lb.
13	2	24–31	H-4 lb.	W-15 lb.	A-1 lb.
14	2	24–31	H-4 lb.	W-17½ lb.	A-1 lb.
15	2	24–30	H-4 lb.	W-17½ lb.	A-2 lb.

PROGRAM 3. Super Fitness PowerWalking for a 200-Pound Man 29 Years of Age or Younger

Week (3 times per week minimum)	Distance (in miles)	Time Allowed (recommended guidelines in minutes)	Extra Weights (H=hand weights W=waist belt A=ankle weights)		
1	½	6–10	H-3 lb.		
2	1	12–15	H-3 lb.		
3	1	12–14	H-3 lb.		
4	1	12–14	H-3 lb.	W-5 lb.	
5	1½	20–25	H-3 lb.	W-5 lb.	
6	1½	20–25	H-4 lb.	W-10 lb.	
7	1½	19–24	H-4 lb.	W-10 lb.	
8	1½	19–24	H-4 lb.	W-12½ lb.	
9	1½	18–23	H-4 lb.	W-12½ lb.	
10	1½	18–23	H-4 lb.	W-15 lb.	
11	2	25–32	H-4 lb.	W-15 lb.	
12	2	25–32	H-5 lb.	W-15 lb.	A-1 lb.
13	2	24–31	H-5 lb.	W-15 lb.	A-1 lb.
14	2	24–31	H-5 lb.	W-17½ lb.	A-2½ lb.
15	2	24–30	H-5 lb.	W-20 lb.	A-2½ lb.

PROGRAM 4. Super Fitness PowerWalking for a 150-Pound Man 30 to 50 Years of Age

Week (3 times per week minimum)	Distance (in miles)	Time Allowed (recommended guidelines in minutes)	Extra Weight (H=hand weights W=waist belt A=ankle weights)		
1	½	7–11	H-1 lb.		
2	1	14–18	H-1 lb.		
3	1	13–17	H-1 lb.		
4	1	13–17	H-1 lb.	W-5 lb.	
5	1½	21–26	H-1 lb.	W-5 lb.	
6	1½	21–26	H-2 lb.	W-5 lb.	
7	1½	20–25	H-2 lb.	W-5 lb.	
8	1½	20–25	H-2 lb.	W-10 lb.	
9	1½	19–24	H-2 lb.	W-10 lb.	
10	1½	19–24	H-3 lb.	W-10 lb.	
11	2	26–33	H-3 lb.	W-10 lb.	
12	2	26–33	H-3 lb.	W-10 lb.	A-1 lb.
13	2	25–32	H-3 lb.	W-10 lb.	A-1 lb.
14	2	25–31	H-3 lb.	W-15 lb.	A-1 lb.
15	2	24–30	H-3 lb.	W-15 lb.	A-1 lb.

PROGRAM 5. Super Fitness PowerWalking for a 175-Pound Man 30 to 50 Years of Age

Week (3 times per week minimum)	Distance (in miles)	Time Allowed (recommended guidelines in minutes)	Extra Weights (H=hand weights W=waist belt A=ankle weights)		
1	½	7−11	H-1 lb.		
2	1	14−18	H-1 lb.		
3	1	13−17	H-1 lb.		
4	1	13−17	H-2 lb.	W-5 lb.	
5	1½	21−26	H-2 lb.	W-5 lb.	
6	1½	21−26	H-2 lb.	W-10 lb.	
7	1½	20−25	H-2 lb.	W-10 lb.	
8	1½	20−25	H-3 lb.	W-10 lb.	
9	1½	19−24	H-3 lb.	W-10 lb.	
10	1½	19−24	H-3 lb.	W-15 lb.	
11	2	26−33	H-3 lb.	W-15 lb.	
12	2	26−33	H-3 lb.	W-15 lb.	A-1 lb.
13	2	25−32	H-3 lb.	W-15 lb.	A-1 lb.
14	2	25−31	H-4 lb.	W-15 lb.	A-1 lb.
15	2	24−30	H-4 lb.	W-17½ lb.	A-1 lb.

PROGRAM 6. Super Fitness PowerWalking for a 200-Pound Man 30 to 50 Years of Age

Week (3 times per week minimum)	Distance (in miles)	Time Allowed (recommended guidelines in minutes)	Extra Weight (H=hand weights W=waist belt A=ankle weights)		
1	½	7−11	H-2 lb.		
2	1	14−18	H-2 lb.		
3	1	13−17	H-2 lb.		
4	1	13−17	H-3 lb.	W-5 lb.	
5	1½	21−26	H-3 lb.	W-5 lb.	
6	1½	21−26	H-3 lb.	W-10 lb.	
7	1½	20−25	H-3 lb.	W-10 lb.	
8	1½	20−25	H-3 lb.	W-15 lb.	
9	1½	19−24	H-3 lb.	W-15 lb.	
10	1½	19−24	H-4 lb.	W-15 lb.	
11	2	26−33	H-4 lb.	W-15 lb.	
12	2	26−33	H-4 lb.	W-15 lb.	A-1 lb.
13	2	25−32	H-4 lb.	W-17½ lb.	A-1 lb.
14	2	25−31	H-5 lb.	W-17½ lb.	A-1 lb.
15	2	24−30	H-5 lb.	W-20 lb.	A-2 lb.

PROGRAM 7. Super Fitness PowerWalking for a 150-Pound Man 50 Years of Age or Older

Week (3 times per week minimum)	Distance (in miles)	Time Allowed (recommended guidelines in minutes)	Extra Weight (H=hand weights W=waist belt A=ankle weights)		
1	½	8–12	H-1 lb.		
2	½	8–10	H-1 lb.		
3	½	7–11	H-1 lb.		
4	1	15–20	H-1 lb.		
5	1	15–20	H-1 lb.	W-5 lb.	
6	1	14–19	H-1 lb.	W-5 lb.	
7	1	13–18	H-2 lb.	W-5 lb.	
8	1½	22–27	H-2 lb.	W-5 lb.	
9	1½	22–27	H-2 lb.	W-10 lb.	
10	1½	21–26	H-2 lb.	W-10 lb.	
11	1½	20–25	H-2 lb.	W-10 lb.	
12	1½	20–25	H-2 lb.	W-10 lb.	A-1 lb.
13	2	27–32	H-2 lb.	W-10 lb.	A-1 lb.
14	2	26–31	H-2 lb.	W-10 lb.	A-1 lb.
15	2	26–31	H-3 lb.	W-15 lb.	A-1 lb.

PROGRAM 8. Super Fitness PowerWalking for a 175-Pound Man 50 Years of Age or Older

Week (3 times per week minimum)	Distance (in miles)	Time Allowed (recommended guidelines in minutes)	Extra Weight (H=hand weights W=waist belt A=ankle weights)		
1	½	8–12	H-1 lb.		
2	½	8–10	H-1 lb.		
3	½	7–11	H-1 lb.		
4	1	15–20	H-1 lb.		
5	1	15–20	H-2 lb.	W-5 lb.	
6	1	14–19	H-2 lb.	W-5 lb.	
7	1	13–18	H-2 lb.	W-5 lb.	
8	1½	22–27	H-3 lb.	W-5 lb.	
9	1½	22–27	H-3 lb.	W-10 lb.	
10	1½	21–26	H-3 lb.	W-10 lb.	
11	1½	20–25	H-3 lb.	W-10 lb.	
12	1½	20–25	H-3 lb.	W-10 lb.	A-1 lb.
13	2	27–32	H-3 lb.	W-10 lb.	A-1 lb.
14	2	26–31	H-3 lb.	W-10 lb.	A-1 lb.
15	2	26–31	H-3 lb.	W-15 lb.	A-1 lb.

PROGRAM 9. Super Fitness PowerWalking for a 200-Pound Man 50 Years of Age or Older

Week (3 times per week minimum)	Distance (in miles)	Time Allowed (recommended guidelines in minutes)	Extra Weight (H=hand weights W=waist belt A=ankle weights)		
1	½	8–12	H-1 lb.		
2	½	8–10	H-1 lb.		
3	½	7–11	H-1 lb.		
4	1	15–20	H-1 lb.		
5	1	15–20	H-1 lb.	W-5 lb.	
6	1	14–19	H-2 lb.	W-5 lb.	
7	1	13–18	H-2 lb.	W-5 lb.	
8	1½	22–27	H-2 lb.	W-5 lb.	
9	1½	22–27	H-2 lb.	W-10 lb.	
10	1½	21–26	H-2 lb.	W-10 lb.	
11	1½	20–25	H-3 lb.	W-10 lb.	
12	1½	20–25	H-3 lb.	W-15 lb.	A-1 lb.
13	2	27–32	H-3 lb.	W-15 lb.	A-1 lb.
14	2	26–31	H-3 lb.	W-15 lb.	A-1 lb.
15	2	26–31	H-3 lb.	W-15 lb.	A-2 lb.

PROGRAM 10. Super Fitness PowerWalking for a 135-Pound Woman 29 Years of Age or Younger

Week (3 times per week minimum)	Distance (in miles)	Time Allowed (recommended guidelines in minutes)	Extra Weight (H=hand weights W=waist belt A=ankle weights)		
1	½	8–11	H-1 lb.		
2	½	7–10	H-1 lb.		
3	1	15–19	H-1 lb.		
4	1	14–18	H-1 lb.	W-5 lb.	
5	1	13–17	H-1 lb.	W-5 lb.	
6	1	12–16	H-2 lb.	W-5 lb.	
7	1½	22–26	H-2 lb.	W-5 lb.	
8	1½	21–25	H-2 lb.	W-7½ lb.	
9	1½	20–24	H-2 lb.	W-7½ lb.	
10	1½	19–23	H-2 lb.	W-7½ lb.	
11	1½	18–22	H-3 lb.	W-10 lb.	
12	1½	18–22	H-3 lb.	W-10 lb.	A-1 lb.
13	2	26–31	H-3 lb.	W-10 lb.	A-1 lb.
14	2	25–30	H-3 lb.	W-10 lb.	A-1 lb.
15	2	24–29	H-3 lb.	W-10 lb.	A-1 lb.

PROGRAM 11. Super Fitness PowerWalking for 135-Pound Woman 30 to 50 Years of Age or Older

Week (3 times per week minimum)	Distance (in miles)	Time Allowed (recommended guidelines in minutes)	Extra Weight (H=hand weights W=waist belt A=ankle weights)		
1	½	8–12	H-1 lb.		
2	½	8–10	H-1 lb.		
3	1	17–21	H-1 lb.		
4	1	16–21	H-1 lb.		
5	1	15–20	H-1 lb.		
6	1	15–20	H-1 lb.	W-5 lb.	
7	1	14–19	H-1 lb.	W-5 lb.	
8	1	13–18	H-1 lb.	W-5 lb.	
9	1½	23–28	H-2 lb.	W-5 lb.	
10	1½	22–27	H-2 lb.	W-5 lb.	
11	1½	21–26	H-2 lb.	W-5 lb.	
12	1½	21–26	H-2 lb.	W-7½ lb.	
13	2	28–33	H-2 lb.	W-7½ lb.	A-1 lb.
14	2	27–32	H-2 lb.	W-7½ lb.	A-1 lb.
15	2	26–31	H-2 lb.	W-7½ lb.	A-1 lb.

PROGRAM 12. Super Fitness PowerWalking for a 135-Pound Woman 50 Years of Age or Older

Week (3 times per week minimum)	Distance (in miles)	Time Allowed (recommended guidelines in minutes)	Extra Weight (H=hand weights W=waist belt A=ankle weights)		
1	½	9–14	H-1 lb.		
2	½	9–13	H-1 lb.		
3	½	8–12	H-1 lb.		
4	1	18–23	H-1 lb.		
5	1	17–22	H-1 lb.		
6	1	16–21	H-1 lb.	W-5 lb.	
7	1	15–20	H-2 lb.	W-5 lb.	
8	1	14–19	H-2 lb.	W-5 lb.	
9	1½	24–29	H-2 lb.	W-5 lb.	
10	1½	23–28	H-2 lb.	W-5 lb.	
11	1½	22–27	H-2 lb.	W-5 lb.	
12	1½	22–27	H-2 lb.	W-7½ lb.	
13	1½	21–26	H-2 lb.	W-7½ lb.	
14	2	30–35	H-2 lb.	W-7½ lb.	A-1 lb.
15	2	28–33	H-2 lb.	W-7½ lb.	A-1 lb.

ALTER YOUR STRIDE FOR FITNESS

An excellent alternative for people who want to add variety to their advanced PowerWalking programs is to vary the medium they walk on. Personally, I've found that both sand and water work well. In the water I always PowerWalk at a depth up to my knees. The resistance posed by both water and sand increases the intensity of the exercise. Another method I use for increasing the intensity of my PowerWalking and for adding variety to my program is to PowerWalk backward against the resistance provided by a partner. My partner exerts pressure against my shoulders with his hands while I Power-Walk backward toward him. Although intense, the pressure is not great enough to prevent me from moving at a brisk pace.

PowerWalking in sand.

Toning Up
and Looking Good

As a former Mr. Universe, I'm a firm believer in the value of weight training as a conditioning technique. I also realize that you don't have to be a competitive athlete or lifter to benefit from weight training. All you really need is a desire to be fit and look fit. Since your muscles constitute 35 to 45 percent of your body weight, firming your muscles will produce a "leaner" look. Your clothes will fit better. You will feel better about yourself because you will look better. You should ignore the misunderstandings surrounding weight training. If you've ever suffered a sore muscle or an aching back, or if you've ever had a pair of jeans that fit more snugly than you wished, then weight training can be a terrific form of exercise for you.

In my teens, I didn't know too much about weight training. I had fantastically developed legs from riding my bicycle up the hills in Oakland, California, but my upper body was only average, despite the fact that I was the arm wrestling champion in my neighborhood. I had never trained with weights. Then one day on my paper route, I met a young man named Joe Gambino. He beat me in an arm wrestling bout, despite the fact that Joe was only 5'5'', a full seven inches shorter than I. Joe invited me over to his house where I discovered the reason for his prowess—a home gym in his garage.

We quickly became close friends, and in the next few months I trained with Joe's weights regularly in his homemade gym. Within three months, I put on over 30 pounds of solid muscle. I became hooked on the value of training with weights. Today, I regularly include a weight-training workout in my conditioning program. The value of a firm and taut body is as important to me in my fifties as it was in my teens.

Although my PowerWalking program contributes to the development of every basic component of fitness, I frequently find it desirable to supplement my conditioning program with a brief, intense program of weight training. As I've said, such a program tones up the muscles, greatly reduces the chances of being injured in strenuous physical activities, and increases overall feelings of well-being. Simply put, weight training is an excellent tool, and I use it to good advantage.

Unfortunately, weight training is viewed by some people as a form of torture they would do anything to avoid. The mere mention of it conjures up visions of big sweaty hulks who take a masochistic delight in abusing themselves with stacks of iron plates. What people don't realize is that everyone who participates in a physically taxing activity would benefit from a higher level of muscular fitness.

The body of a muscularly fit person is better prepared to withstand physical stresses and, therefore, is less susceptible to injury. For example, because the knees are stabilized by the combined efforts of the front thigh muscles and rear thigh muscles, strengthening these muscles reduces the likelihood of incurring a knee injury. Given the physical demands that athletes place on their bodies, it's hardly surprising that so many of them get injured. But injuries do *not* have to be an unavoidable by-product of strenuous physical activity.

The consensus of most of the top sports medicine physicians is that more than half the injuries that occur during sports — including jogging and running — could easily be prevented through proper weight training. Quite simply, a stronger thigh muscle is less susceptible to pulls and strains, a stronger tendon less likely to become inflamed (tendonitis), a stronger front, lower leg muscle less prone to shin splints, and so forth.

Physicians who advise you to refrain from engaging in weight-training programs do not understand what *proper* weight training is and the benefits that can be derived from it. They argue that weight training decreases your flexibility, creates a strength imbalance in the antagonistic, or opposing, muscles of the body, and is obviously unnecessary anyway because so many successful athletes have never trained with weights. They are wrong on all counts.

Because most forms of physical activity do not require the muscles involved to go through their full range of motion, people who do not exercise their muscles in other ways are *less* flexible than those who do. Numerous studies have demonstrated conclusively that proper weight training is a way of increasing such flexibility. Also, normal physical activity, however strenuous, neither adequately develops nor fully maintains the required strength balance between antagonistic pairs of muscles. To maintain proper muscle balance all opposing muscles should generally be equal in strength (with the exception of the quadriceps, which should be about one and a half times as strong as the opposing hamstrings). When you develop muscle imbalance and subsequently place too much stress on the weaker muscle, an injury can result, such as a pull, tear, or strain. A properly designed weight-training program can prevent such imbalances.

As for the many world-class athletes who don't train with weights, they are successful not *because* they don't, but in *spite* of their negligence.The number of world-class athletes who do some weight training has increased dramatically in recent years. But who knows how many potentially successful athletes had their running careers aborted because of a debilitating injury? The injury-free careers of the Bill Rodgerses and Andrea Jaegers of the world is small consolation to the injured weekend athlete.

It is also important to emphasize that a weight program can contribute to improved athletic performance. Obviously, if you're not injured or are injured less frequently, your competitive efforts down the line will get better. Development of your strength through weight training will also improve every aspect of your performance and your body's ability to undergo the stress of competition.

As a result of numerous research studies conducted during the past ten years and subsequent field testing at several universities, a new approach to weight training has been developed. It is based on the premise that a person who wants to gain higher levels of muscular fitness would like to improve as much as possible in the least amount of time, and in the safest possible way. It is also based on the discovery that, when it comes to weight training, *more is not better!*

GUIDELINES FOR WEIGHT USE

Who should train with weights?

Weight training is for anyone interested in being as injury-free as possible.

I often am asked about whether women should train with weights. Without any reservation I respond, absolutely yes. The myth that weight training will somehow dehumanize or defeminize women is no more valid than the belief that women should restrict their occupational roles to the home. What foolishness! Women have just as much to gain from additional levels of strength as do men—if not more. Women's fear that strength training will somehow make them unattractive is also without basis. Women simply do not have the genetic potential to develop large muscles. They secrete a hormone (estrogen) that actually inhibits the development of muscle. Unlike men, who secrete testosterone—a hormone that facilitates the development of muscle—women can't develop large muscles even if they want to. They can, however, gain additional strength. They can trim up their muscles and in the process lose a few unwanted inches around their arms and waist. They can also reduce their chances of suffering an injury. In short, women have everything to gain by weight training.

One of the first world-class women athletes to train with weights on a regular basis was the runner Gayle Barron, who trained on a high-intensity, progressive resistance program prior to winning the 1978 Boston Marathon. People who are over 40 also will benefit greatly from proper weight training. As people get older, they tend to become less flexible. Weight training can reverse this loss and make physical activity a more enjoyable, less injurious activity.

Which exercises should be performed?

Precisely which exercises should be performed depends greatly on the equipment available. Regardless of the equipment used, an effective weight-training program should include at least one exercise (and usually two) for each of the five major muscle groups in the body: the muscles of the lower back and buttocks, legs, torso, arms, and abdominal region. In addition to these "core" exercises, two or three exercises specific to the demands imposed by the activity (for example, for runners an exercise for developing the groin muscles) should be included. The complete program would involve ten to twelve exercises, as shown in the Sample Strength-Training

Sample Strength-Training Program for PowerWalkers

Free Weights	Nautilus	Muscles Developed	Action of Muscles	Fitness Basis for Exercise
Squat	Leg extension	Quadriceps	Extend lower leg	Eliminates frontal thigh pulls
Straight-legged dead lift	Hip and back	Buttocks, lower back	Extend the spine, lateral flexion of the spine, extend upper leg	Eliminates lower back-related problems
Buddy leg curl	Leg curl	Hamstrings	Extend and flex upper leg, flex lower leg	Eliminates rear thigh pulls
Buddy leg raise	Abductor-adductor	Adductor magnus, gluteus medius (buttocks, groin)	Adduct and abduct the leg	Eliminates groin pulls
Side lateral raise	Double shoulder (lateral raise)	Deltoids (shoulder)	Raise, lower, and rotate arm	Eliminates shoulder-related problems
Seated press behind neck	Double shoulder (seated press)	Deltoids, triceps	Raise, lower, and rotate arm	Eliminates shoulder-related problems
Bent-over row	Pullover	Latissimus dorsi (side-back)	Move arm down and backward, stabilize torso	Eliminates lat pulls, stabilizes shoulder, assists in action involved in running hills
Biceps curl	Biceps curl	Biceps	Flex the arm	Assists in holding arm comfortably at proper angle
Bench triceps extension	Triceps extension	Triceps	Extend the arm	Assists in holding arm comfortably at proper angle
Curl-ups	Abdominal machine	Rectus abdominus, transversals (abdomen)	Flex spine, stabilize posture	Assists breathing by stabilizing rib cage
Buddy ankle curl	Foot flexion	Tibialis anterior (shin)	Flex and invert foot	Eliminates shin splints

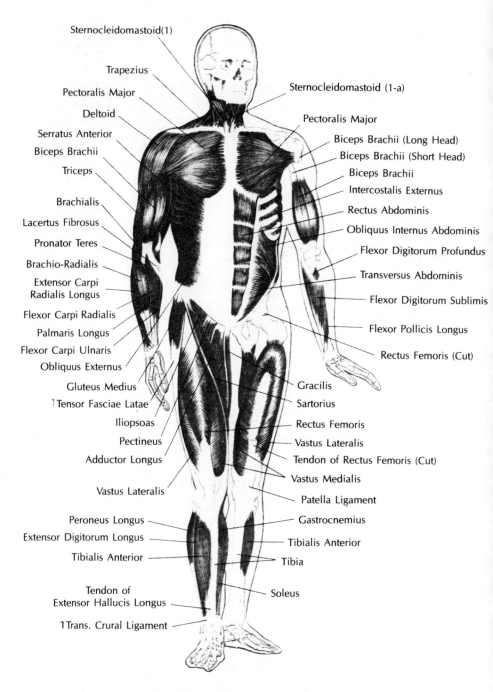

Figure 3. POSTERIOR VIEW OF THE MUSCLES OF THE BODY.
Reprinted by permission of Cramer Products Inc.

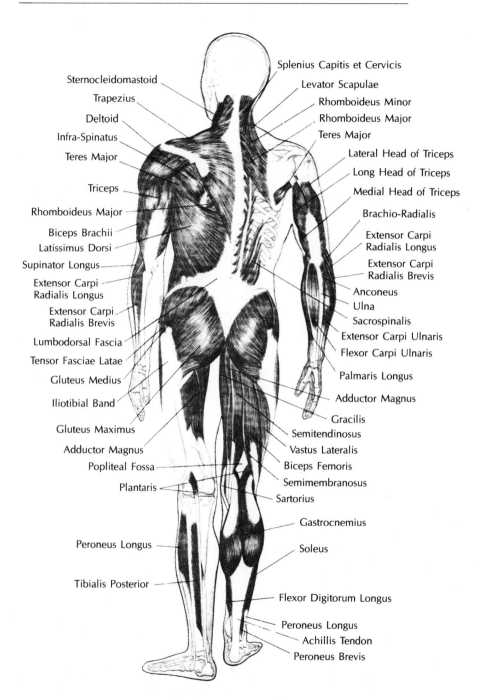

Sternocleidomastoid
Trapezius
Deltoid
Infra-Spinatus
Teres Major
Triceps
Rhomboideus Major
Biceps Brachii
Latissimus Dorsi
Supinator Longus
Extensor Carpi Radialis Longus
Extensor Carpi Radialis Brevis
Lumbodorsal Fascia
Tensor Fasciae Latae
Gluteus Medius
Iliotibial Band
Gluteus Maximus
Adductor Magnus
Popliteal Fossa
Plantaris
Peroneus Longus
Tibialis Posterior

Splenius Capitis et Cervicis
Levator Scapulae
Rhomboideus Minor
Rhomboideus Major
Teres Major
Lateral Head of Triceps
Long Head of Triceps
Medial Head of Triceps
Brachio-Radialis
Extensor Carpi Radialis Longus
Extensor Carpi Radialis Brevis
Anconeus
Ulna
Sacrospinalis
Extensor Carpi Ulnaris
Flexor Carpi Ulnaris
Palmaris Longus
Adductor Magnus
Gracilis
Semitendinosus
Vastus Lateralis
Biceps Femoris
Semimembranosus
Sartorius
Gastrocnemius
Soleus
Flexor Digitorum Longus
Peroneus Longus
Achillis Tendon
Peroneus Brevis

Figure 4. MUSCLES OF THE BODY: ANTERIOR VIEW.

Reprinted by permission of Cramer Products, Inc.

Strength-Training Exercises by Muscle Group and Equipment

	Free Weights	Multi-Station Equipment	Variable Resistance Equipment
Buttocks/lower back	Squat Stiff-legged deadlift	Leg press Hyperextension	Hip and back Leg press
Quadriceps	Squat	Leg extension Leg press	Leg extension Leg press
Hamstrings	Squat	Leg curl Leg press	Leg curl Leg press
Calves	Calf raise	Toe press on leg press	Calf raise on multi-exercise Toe press on leg press
Latissimus dorsi	Bent-over rowing Bent-armed pullover Stiff-armed pullover	Chin-up Pull down on lat machine	Pullover Behind neck Torso/arm Chin-up on multi-exercise
Trapezius	Shoulder shrug Dumbbell shoulder shrug	Shoulder shrug	Neck and shoulder Rowing torso
Deltoids	Press, press behind neck Upright rowing, forward raise Side raise with dumbbells	Seated press Upright rowing	Double shoulder 1. lateral raise 2. overhead press Rowing torso
Pectoralis majors	Bench press Dumbbell flies	Bench press Parallel dip	Double chest 1. arm cross 2. decline press Parallel dip on multi-exercise
Biceps	Standing curl	Curl Chin-up	Compound curl Biceps curl Multi-curl
Triceps	Triceps extension with dumbbells	Press down on lat machine	Compound triceps Triceps extension Multi-triceps
Forearms	Wrist curl	Wrist curl	Wrist curl on multi-exercise
Abdominals/obliques	Sit-up Side bend with dumbbells	Sit-up Leg raise	Sit-up on multi-exercise Leg raise on multi-exercise Side bend on multi-exercise
Neck	Neck bridge (dangerous)	Neck harness	4-way neck Rotary neck Neck and shoulder

Program table on page 149. A description of each of these exercises is presented later in this chapter. The muscles of the body are illustrated in Figures 3 and 4. The basic strength-training exercises that can be performed to develop the major muscles are given in the table on page 152, which lists strength-training exercises by muscle group.

What kind of equipment is required?

A great many tools exist for developing muscular fitness; for example, resistance calisthenics, free weights (available at many sporting goods stores for under $100), and specialized machines such as Nautilus and Universal Gym equipment. To be effective, the equipment must place a demand on the muscle. In recent years, a number of innovative modifications have been made to make strength-training equipment more productive. The most effective of the new devices are the Nautilus and Universal variable resistance machines, which became very popular during the past decade. You should keep in mind, however, that *it is not the tool but the way you use it that is the most important factor in developing muscular fitness.* Formal equipment is not even necessary if you have a rudimentary knowledge of how the body works and, in some instances, a partner who can provide the resistance during a workout.

What are resistance calisthenics?

Developed originally in an effort to find a way to make people strong enough to handle their own body weight, resistance calisthenics are exercises that enable you to develop muscular fitness at your own pace. Resistance calisthenics offer several advantages: generally, no equipment is involved; they can be performed by anyone at any age and at any level of fitness; they can be done anywhere (in the home, outdoors, or at a gym); and they produce results in a relatively short period of time. There are three basic forms of resistance calisthenics:

negative-only exercises, buddy (partner) exercises, and stick exercises.

Negative-only exercises are those in which you perform only the negative (eccentric or lowering) phase of an exercise. For example, when performing a negative-only push-up, you lower yourself to the floor from a front-leaning-rest position taking approximately 5 seconds. Once you've lowered yourself down, return to the starting position by first assuming a knees-on-the-ground position and then repeat the lowering phase.

Buddy exercises are those in which you perform a specific movement (for example, a side lateral raise with your arms) against resistance provided by your partner. The amount of pressure applied should be what will enable you to complete each phase of the exercise (extension and contraction) in approximately 3 seconds.

Stick exercises are essentially another form of buddy exercise except that you move a stick, while holding both ends, through a specific range of motion. Your partner exerts pressure against the stick. I recommend using the handle of a plumber's helper for the stick.

For best results I suggest doing a combination of the negative-only, buddy, and stick exercises. A complete description of such manual resistance exercises is provided in Dan Riley's book, *Maximum Muscular Fitness: Strength Training Without Weights* (West Point, NY: Leisure Press, 1982).

In what order should the exercises be performed?

Some authorities on fitness suggest that exercises which develop the largest muscles should be done first. Because the smaller muscles are needed to assist in exercises aimed at fatiguing larger muscles (such as the seated press in which the forearm flexors assist larger shoulder and back muscles), it is counterproductive to fatigue the smaller muscles first. Experts generally recommend that exercises for specific body regions should be performed in the following order: lower back and buttocks, legs, torso, arms, abdominal area, and (if included) neck. I personally recommend that the body parts be exercised as follows: shoulders, chest, upper back, biceps, triceps, legs, lower back, abdominal area, and neck. My theory is that the legs, buttocks, and abdominal region should be worked last because they are the foundation and supporting muscles of the body. Try both methods and see which works best for you.

How many times should exercises be done?

Each time a specific exercise is done it is called a repetition, or *rep*. A predetermined number of repetitions performed continuously without resting is a *set*. It would be a lifetime task to list the program variations derived over the years regarding how many reps and sets should be performed. The traditional DeLorme theory mandates that strength is developed by doing three sets of five to eight reps, and muscular endurance by performing three sets of nine to fifteen reps. In recent years, however, several studies have proven that one set of eight to twelve reps performed to a point of maximum muscular fatigue is sufficient to realize both goals. Further repetitions, even after a rest period, provide no additional benefits. It is also more productive psychologically to perform a single bout of intense effort.

How much weight should be lifted?

Broad variations exist regarding how much weight to lift for an exercise. Most systems involve some predetermined (and totally arbitrary) percentage of perceived maximum level. In other words, a lifter is instructed to perform a given percentage of his or her "perceived maximum ability" to do a single repetition of an exercise. This "percentage of max" system fails to take mental states into consideration. On some days, you feel like you can do everything—and therefore you can. On other days you feel less confident and cannot do as much. Therefore, the most effective system for identifying how much to lift is to use a weight that will permit at least eight, but no more than twelve, repetitions of a specific exercise. If eight reps cannot be performed, then the weight is too heavy. If more than twelve reps can be done, then it is too light. When starting a program, a lifter should select a weight well within his or her capabilities and then work up to an appropriate level of resistance within three to five workouts.

At what speed should exercises be performed?

Slowly! Each repetition of an exercise should take about 5 seconds — 2 seconds on the positive (lifting) phase and 3 seconds on the negative (lowering) phase. While a weight could obviously be moved through the positive phase faster, to do so would involve throwing or jerking it. As a result, only those muscle fibers required for momentum would benefit from the exercise. Explosively throwing or jerking a weight also puts additional stress on the skeletal joints. When the exercise is done correctly, the muscles are forced to work continuously throughout. Five-second repetitions place the emphasis in weight training where it should be — on building strength, *not* demonstrating it. Accordingly, a complete set of eight to twelve repetitions should take about 40 to 60 seconds.

How much time should elapse between exercises?

No scientifically documented information exists regarding how much time should be allotted between various exercises. However, 15 to 60 seconds is the recommended guideline. Performing ten to twelve exercises lasting 40 to 60 seconds each, with 15 to 60 seconds rest intervals between each exercise, translates into a weight-training workout of about 15 to 25 minutes. No additional time is necessary. If you want to receive an aerobic benefit from your weight-training workout, as well as have an effect on your muscular fitness level, you should reduce the time between each exercise in your workout to 15 seconds or less. In a major study in 1975 conducted at

the U.S. Military Academy, researchers found that intense cir-
cuit weight training (where the work/rest ratio is equal at least
to a 4 to 1 ratio) produces substantial improvement in both a
person's aerobic and muscular fitness levels. If your main goal
is to develop strength, I recommend that you take approximately 60 seconds of rest between exercises.

How much time should elapse between workouts?

Unlike PowerWalking, for example, which many people
undertake five, six, or even seven days a week, weight training
requires that you provide the body with sufficient rest between
workouts in order to permit it to adapt to the stresses imposed
on it. The recommended rest period is at least 48 hours. Most
weight-training programs involve three workouts per week on
alternating days, with an additional rest day. Recent research
has indicated that, depending on your age, additional rest between workouts may be necessary. The results of one major
study completed last year showed that for people over 30, two
workouts per week produced higher levels of muscular fitness
than did the traditional three. It is also a generally accepted
rule to allow no more than 96 hours to lapse between workouts.

When should training be done?

If possible, an intense weight-training session and a highly
rigorous athletic bout should not be scheduled on the same
days. If they must be conducted on the same day, one should
be done in the morning and the other in the evening. If you
must do both workouts consecutively, I recommend that you
do the weight training first, followed by the PowerWalking. On
the other hand, if you are training for an athletic event, I recommend that you practice the athletic skills specific to your
sport before your weight-training workout.

How should the weights be held?

Depending on your personal viewpoint, one of the major advantages of weight-training machines as a mode for developing muscular fitness is the fact that there is a specific place to put your hands while performing each exercise. When exercising with free weights (barbells and dumbbells), on the other hand, there are four grips that can be used: the overhand, the underhand, the alternate, and the false grip. The *overhand grip* is the most widely used grip when performing the barbell exercises. The thumbs are hooked underneath the bar with the knuckles placed on top of the bar. When the *underhand grip* is used, the thumbs are hooked above the bar and the knuckles are placed underneath the bar. When using the *alternate grip,* a combination of the overhand and the underhand grip is used. One hand is placed above and one hand below the bar. The alternate grip is the strongest grip of the four. It can be used when performing an exercise similar to the dead lift or shoulder shrug—both are described later. When using the false grip, the thumbs are not hooked around the bar. It is a grip that should not be used by a novice lifter. It can be a substitute for the overhand or underhand grip when performing certain exercises. It is often substituted because it is a more comfortable grip. As its name implies, however, it is not a very safe grip. The width of the particular grip being used varies with the individual and the exercise being performed. The width of the grip should provide the following: (1) maximum range of movement; (2) isolation of the specific muscle or group of muscles being exercised; and (3) comfort.

FREE WEIGHT EXERCISES: STEP BY STEP

SQUAT

With your feet approximately 18 inches apart, the barbell resting on your back behind the neck and your heels elevated approximately 2 or 3 inches, lower your buttocks until the middle of the thigh is parallel to the floor. Pause and return to the starting position. Place a bench behind you and under your buttocks at the lowest position of the movement as a safety measure. Keep your head up and back straight during the exercise.

(A)

Squat

(B)

STRAIGHT-LEGGED DEAD LIFT

With your feet about 18 inches apart, keep your head up and back straight. Lock your knees to keep your legs straight. Grasp the bar, and keeping your legs straight, stand erect and arch your back slightly. Pause and lower the weight slowly.

Straight legged dead lift

(A)

(B)

BUDDY LEG CURL

Lie face down on a bench or on the ground with both legs extended. Your partner places his/her hands behind your left heel. While your partner applies resistance, move your lower leg up toward your back while keeping your upper leg stationary. Move your lower leg as far as is comfortable (but not past the perpendicular). Pause, slowly return to the starting position against your partner's resistance, and repeat. When your left leg is exhausted, perform same exercise with your right leg.

BUDDY LATERAL RAISE

Lie on your side on the ground. Your partner places his/her hands on the side of your outer leg just above the knee. While your partner applies resistance, raise your leg as high as possible, keeping the leg straight. Pause. Your partner then reverses the resistance by placing his hands on the inside of your leg just above the knee. When your partner applies resistance, return to the starting position by pulling your leg downward. Repeat. Then change to the other side and perform the exercise with your other leg.

SIDE LATERAL RAISE

With your feet shoulder-width apart and holding the weight with both arms extended downward, raise the weight until both arms are parallel to the floor. Pause and slowly lower the weight to the starting position.

(A)

Side lateral raise

(B)

BENT ARM FLIES

Lying on your back on a bench with your arms extended over your chest with arms partially bent, slowly lower the dumbbells down to your sides. Pause, then raise the dumbbells to the starting position.

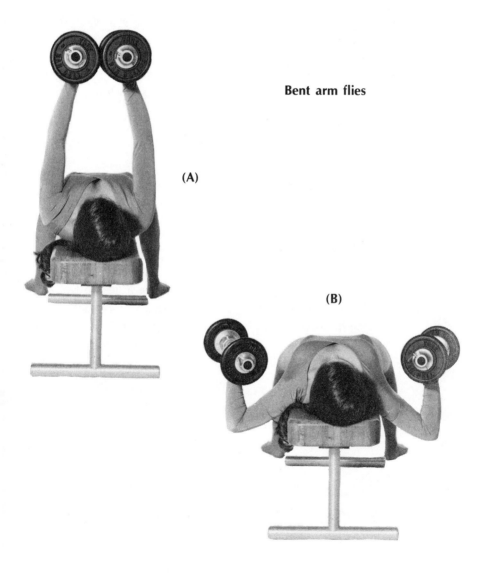

Bent arm flies

(A)

(B)

SEATED PRESS BEHIND NECK

From a seated position with your back straight, start with the bar resting on your shoulders behind the neck. Press the bar straight up, then slowly lower the bar until it touches your shoulders again. As soon as the bar touches the shoulders, repeat the press. Do not rest the bar on your shoulders.

BENCH PRESS

Lie on your back on the bench with your feet flat on the floor. Keep your buttocks flat on the bench. From the arms-extended position, lower the bar as far as possible, pause, and press the bar up to the extended position. Most people use a bench specifically designed to enable the lifter to take the weight from the extended holders while in a prone position. If you don't have such a bench, you'll need a partner.

BENT OVER ROW

Bending at the waist with your back parallel to the floor and feet shoulder-width apart with legs straight, pull the bar up to touch your chest. Pause and slowly lower the weight.

(A)

Bent over row

(B)

BICEPS CURL

Using a straight bar or an E-Z curl bar, stand upright with your feet shoulder-width apart. Raise the bar upward as far as possible without moving your elbows. Pause and slowly lower the bar to the extended position.

(A)

Biceps curl

(B)

BENCH TRICEPS EXTENSION

Lie on your back on a bench with your feet flat on the floor and your arms extended above your chest. Keeping your upper arms vertical, bend your arms at the elbows and slowly lower the bar to the bench just behind your head. Pause, then slowly raise the bar to the starting position, keeping your elbows at shoulder width.

CURL-UPS

Take a seated position with your legs bent at a 90-degree angle to the floor, both feet together. Interlock your hands behind your head and lower your torso until the head is almost touching the floor. Pause and move your torso upward (curl) until it is perpendicular to the floor.

BUDDY ANKLE CURL

Sit on the ground with both legs extended before you and your feet flexed. Your partner applies resistance by holding on to your toes (only) with both hands. While your partner applies resistance, flex your foot toward your body as far as it will go. Pause, slowly return to starting position, and repeat. When one leg is exhausted, repeat the exercise with the other leg.

TOE RAISE

Stand with approximately the front one third of your foot on a pad or board at least 2 inches thick and hold a barbell across your shoulders. Raise your heels off the floor while rising up on your toes. Pause and slowly return to the starting position. Raise your heels as high as possible on each repetition.

(A)

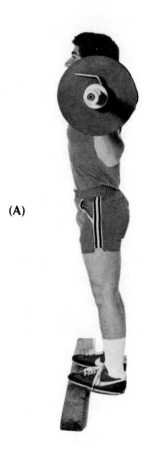

Toe raise

(B)

(C)

VARIABLE RESISTANCE (NAUTILUS) EXERCISES

I recommend that you ask the instructor at your local Nautilus Fitness Center to give you detailed instructions on how to perform each exercise and use each machine properly. Because of the complexity of each machine, space does not permit me to give a detailed explanation in this book on how to perform the various Nautilus exercises.

Weight training can be a valuable addition to your program for developing total physical fitness if you remember the following points:

- Emphasize the proper execution of each exercise. When form is compromised, results are compromised.
- Work to a point of maximum muscular fatigue on every exercise. Intensity has nothing whatsoever to do with the traditional practice of making guttural sounds or working a muscle to a point of catatonic shock. Exercise to a point where a full-range repetition of a specific lift can no longer be done in proper form.
- Emphasize the negative phase of each exercise as much as the positive phase. Perform each repetition through a full range of motion.
- Remember that the purpose of a weight-training workout is to make you more physically fit than you were before the workout. Weight training should not be a competitive contest between individuals or an individual and a machine.
- Set realistic goals. If you engage in a regular program of properly performed total body workouts, you've done your best.
- Keep accurate records of every workout. Records enable you to identify personal progress and problem areas.

11

Questions and Answers About PowerWalking

ver the years, I've had a number of friends and colleagues ask me about certain aspects of PowerWalking. In addition, several months ago, after an article appeared in the *Los Angeles Times*, I received numerous inquiries from interested readers. I've tried to include here many of the questions I feel would be of interest to you.

Q. Is PowerWalking a better activity for women than jogging?
A. Yes. PowerWalking is an exceptionally good exercise for women. Contrary to jogging where a woman's breasts are often injured or tend to shrink because of the constant bouncing that breaks down breast tissues, PowerWalking involves a steady, rhythmic movement that actually firms up the tissues.

Q. How does PowerWalking differ from race walking?
A. Race walking requires considerable practice to learn. Because the techniques of race walking are relatively difficult, many people simply won't devote the time to learn them. I also believe that it's far easier for a person to adjust the intensity (via the six components) of PowerWalking than of race walking. In addition, I personally feel that the ungraceful feeling one gets when race walking (because of the extreme hip swivel motion) will be a deterrent to most people. If they feel they look foolish, they won't commit themselves to race walking on a regular basis.

PowerWalking is excellent exercise for women.

Q. Will PowerWalking give you instant fitness?
A. No, nothing can do that. I can assure you, however, that within a month, PowerWalking three times a week, at least 15 minutes a session, will produce dramatic results.

Q. Will PowerWalking improve your aerobic (heart-lung) fitness?
A. Yes. PowerWalking increases oxygen intake and improves your circulation. You have nearly 60,000 miles of blood vessels, mostly capillaries, which bring oxygen to your muscles. Only a few of these capillaries are open when your muscles are not in use. Nearly 50 times as many will open when your muscles are involved with exercise. When you are PowerWalking, the leg muscle contractions compress the veins, thereby improving the return of blood from the lower extremities. This blood must flow back to the heart against the pull of gravity. When you improve the muscles of your legs, you will also improve the pumping action provided by these muscles. As a result, your circulation will be improved.

Q. Will PowerWalking improve my posture?
A. Yes. When you PowerWalk, you walk erect. You don't lean forward. Your shoulders are laid back, but not forced back. The muscular tone provided, as well as the time spent concentrating on proper postural alignment, will help your posture.

Q. At what time of day should I PowerWalk?
A. Whenever you feel like it and your schedule permits. Some people like to PowerWalk before bedtime. They feel that a brisk PowerWalk before bed is a more effective sleep inducer than a sleeping pill, a drink, or the late-late show. Others like to start the day with a PowerWalk, because they feel that it energizes them and lets them start the day feeling fresh and alive. Personally, I don't have a favorite time. I like to Power-Walk anytime.

Q. Once I work my way up to the advanced PowerWalking program, do I have to wear ankle weights? I have weak ankles and don't like to use ankle weights.
A. No. The use and placement of additional weights is optional.

Q. I love the outdoors. Can PowerWalking get you in shape for other activities?
A. Most certainly. Since PowerWalking enables you to develop all-around fitness, it can be a valuable conditioner for any activity that involves physical exertion. Many of my friends love to hike, for example, and use PowerWalking to condition themselves for the long treks through the hinterlands. I feel that PowerWalking is also an excellent conditioner for the weekend athlete—someone who plays tennis or golf on weekends but needs something during the week to help maintain a proper level of fitness. A far more unusual example of the value of PowerWalking was recently provided by a friend of my wife who used PowerWalking to condition and prepare herself for surgery.

Q. Do you PowerWalk on rainy days?
A. Yes. Sometimes I ignore the rain or let it serve as part of my effort to mobile meditate—I just PowerWalk in the rain! At other times, I PowerWalk indoors to the sounds of music. PowerWalking to a John Philip Sousa record is my personal favorite indoor version.

Q. Is it safe to PowerWalk at high altitudes?
A. Yes, but it is important to remember that your body works somewhat less efficiently at high altitudes. Accordingly, you'll have to PowerWalk at a considerably lower level of intensity for the first three or four days when exercising at high altitudes.

Q. Can I PowerWalk in the snow?
A. It depends on the depth of the snow and your willingness to subject yourself to the hazards of inclement weather. I have a friend in Colorado who PowerWalks in the snow using snow-shoes!

Q. My friend and I have both been PowerWalking for almost seven months, yet he is able to do more than I can. Is there something wrong with me?
A. No, your goal should be to improve yourself. Don't compare yourself with anyone else. Concern yourself with building fitness, not demonstrating it.

Q. Is any special equipment required for PowerWalking?
A. Generally no. The only requirements are a pair of shoes that fit and, if you get involved with the advanced PowerWalking program, extra weight in a form you can use.

Q. How will I know when I'm super fit?
A. When mountains feel like hills and hills feel like you are PowerWalking on level terrain, you'll know that you are super fit!

Q. Is there a minimum age for PowerWalking?
A. PowerWalking can be done safely all your life, at any age. I personally feel that PowerWalking is a super exercise for kids. It's safe. It doesn't place an abnormal demand on their developing skeletal system. It can be performed anywhere, anytime, by kids regardless of their existing level of fitness. It doesn't eliminate any child from enjoying the activity since there are no "minimum" levels of fitness or ability to meet. PowerWalking is also a great activity for kids because it exposes them to the idea of "total fitness."

People of all ages—kids to seniors—enjoy and benefit from PowerWalking.

Q. How much harder is it to PowerWalk with ankle weights than with weights strapped to the waist?
A. The climbers on the 1953 Mount Everest expedition figured that carrying one pound on the feet was equal to five pounds on the back in terms of physical effort required.

Q. How much more energy would a person expend in PowerWalking up a 10 percent grade?
A. The energy cost of PowerWalking more than doubles on a 10 percent grade.

Q. I commute to work in New York City. Is it beneficial for me to PowerWalk the eight blocks from my subway exit to my office? Is there a minimum amount of time that should be spent PowerWalking?
A. It depends on what you expect and need from PowerWalking. From an aerobic standpoint, you need to PowerWalk for a minimum of 15 minutes before any significant improvement will occur. In most instances, I doubt if it will take you 15 minutes to walk eight blocks. There are other benefits, however, to be gained from PowerWalking eight blocks. As I indicated in Chapter 8, mobile meditating while PowerWalking is an excellent technique for clearing your mind and helping you relax. This may be just the thing you need before you start your workday. On the way home, mobile meditating may help reduce the tensions that may have built up during the day. Another advantage of PowerWalking the eight blocks is that you'll burn up additional calories. On a 10-minute PowerWalk, you could expend as many as 150 calories. Those could be the 150 calories you eat during your 10 a.m. snack. One final advantage of PowerWalking, even for a short distance, is that PowerWalking helps unlimber your muscles—muscles that usually tighten up overnight. Try it. You'll feel great.

Q. Will I be able to eat more once I have lost my excess fat?
A. Yes, more calories are used to maintain a muscular body than a fat one. Even when you sleep, your muscles burn calories. Fat doesn't.

Q. Are there more walkers or joggers in America?
A. According to a national adult physical fitness survey conducted recently, the adults who walk for exercise outnumber the joggers more than six to one.

Q. For city dwellers, is there a trade-off between the benefits gained from performing vigorous aerobic exercise outdoors and inhaling the polluted air? When I deep breathe while PowerWalking, will I suffer more from the polluted air?
A. There's no doubt that inhaling clean air is far better than breathing in the somewhat polluted air of our traffic-congested cities. However, the benefits of PowerWalking far outweigh any possible limitations from inhaling urban air. The only exception to this, in my opinion, is the greater metropolitan Los Angeles area on severe smog alert days.

Q. Should I refrain from PowerWalking when I'm pregnant?
A. *Absolutely not,* unless your doctor is aware of a specific reason you should refrain from rigorous exercise during that period. Fortunately, more and more physicians are becoming aware of the benefits of high levels of physical fitness for women during their pregnancy. Numerous studies have indicated that the more physically fit woman has fewer difficulties during delivery, recovers more quickly to her normal patterns of living, and generally has fewer problems of any kind during her pregnancy than the less fit mother-to-be. Women who are pregnant frequently exercise well into their eighth month of pregnancy. PowerWalking is a super exercise for "keeping Mama fit."

Q. *As a sophomore in high school, I really enjoy playing sports and would do almost anything within my power to be a better athlete. Will PowerWalking help me to achieve my goal? I'm confused, since all great athletes seem to use so many different systems.*

A. Obviously, since many excellent athletes use different programs, you may assume that there are many roads to success. I firmly believe that PowerWalking is the best system if your goal is to develop total fitness in the fastest and safest way possible. Regardless of the system, you should remember that there are some fundamentals that any successful program must have.

Pregnant women find PowerWalking—with a doctor's permission—an ideal exercise form.

First, the developmental program must place a demand on the system of the body you want to improve. No demand, no improvement—it's that simple. Second, the program should be based on sound physiological principles so that you don't encounter an undue risk of being injured. Third, the program should be based on a reasonable, graduated level of improvement. You don't get "into" or "out of" shape overnight. Fourth, the program should feature a scientifically sound mix of rest, proper nutrition, and exercise. Unfortunately, many great athletes do not follow programs based on these principles. Since they are neurologically gifted, such athletes are successful not because of their training programs, but in spite of them.

Q. I'm in my fifties and sometimes I suffer sore muscles during my first few training workouts. What should I do if I develop soreness from PowerWalking? My wife suggests that I use DMSO. Do you concur?
A. DMSO is dimethyl sulfoxide. It is a controversial drug that has recently been acclaimed as a wonder drug for athletic injuries. It has been used for years as an industrial solvent. Applied topically, it has helped sprained ankles and caused soreness problems to heal faster, according to some people. Others have stated they weren't able to detect any noticeable difference by using DMSO. Most states do not allow pharmacies to sell DMSO because it has yet to be approved by the Federal Drug Administration. I feel that more research is needed before an appropriate conclusion can be made as to its benefits. As for your specific needs, I recommend that you stretch extensively both before and after your PowerWalk. I personally have never gotten sore from PowerWalking. If for some reason you do, cut back on your program slightly. You may be trying to do too much too soon.

Q. If something hurts while I'm PowerWalking, and I continue working out anyway, won't I get tougher?

A. Not necessarily. While exercising, if you experience some discomfort, you should reduce the level of your effort and give it 5 to 10 minutes. If after that period, the pain has disappeared, then resume your normal workout. If, however, the pain is constant or has increased—stop! You should not exercise through pain. Exercising through pain only increases the likelihood that you will be injured. Also, if you continue training while in pain, your body will naturally compensate for the painful area and assume an abnormal pattern of movement. This will undoubtedly lead to secondary problems. One of the most difficult tasks facing athletes of any age is learning the difference between pain and discomfort. Pain is your body's way of telling you that something is seriously amiss. Discomfort is usually a signal that you are placing a greater demand on a system than you normally do.

Q. I never seem to have a good feeling for how much water I should drink before or after PowerWalking. Is thirst a good indicator of my need for water?

A. Only in some instances. In most instances, thirst is generally not a sensitive indicator of an individual's need for additional water. Prior to an athletic contest, for example, an athlete may be suffering from a substantial lack of body water and still not be thirsty because of the intense emotional atmosphere. A prudent practice is to consume some water periodically whether you feel like you need it or not. You should be particularly aware of your need for water on hot, humid days. On such days, you might actually lose 5 to 10 pounds or more during the course of a 30- to 40-minute PowerWalk. A highly conditioned individual can maintain his body functions at a high level until his water loss equals 4 to 5 percent of his body weight (7½ pounds for a 150-pound person). For those who are not in good condition, the guideline is that human performance will begin to be affected when the loss of body water reaches a level of 3 percent.

Q. Will high-energy capsules, such as those marketed for athletes, offer me an excellent source of energy for Power-Walking?

A. Assuming that such a capsule weighed 5 grams (a huge size for a capsule), the highest number of calories the capsule could provide would be 45 if the capsule were pure fat—the most concentrated form of food energy. Given the daily caloric requirements of the athletically inclined individual (3500 calories plus), 45 calories is a drop in the bucket. In simple terms, such capsules are basically a fraud.

Q. Is there any value in jumping rope in addition to Power-Walking?

A. From a conditioning standpoint, not much. If you jumped rope at a speed that produced an appropriate level of intensity (a heart rate of 145 to 158 beats per minute) for an extended period of time (15 to 20 minutes), there would possibly be a positive effect on the heart-lung complex, provided you engaged in three or more such workouts per week. Since most rope-skipping sessions produce neither result (and *both* are necessary), the main value of rope skipping is the general development of kinesthetic awareness (you develop the ability to know what your feet are doing without looking at them). Given the time and effort involved, rope skipping has, at best, minimal value.

Q. My wife loves to PowerWalk. However, I can't get her interested in weight training. Is there anything I can do to convince her that it is in her best interests to lift weights?

A. Many women, unfortunately, have a serious apprehension about the value and need for training with weights. There is no magic formula or all-persuasive argument for overcoming that concern. When I discuss strength training with women, I always try to emphasize the following points: (1) Strength training will not defeminize them; in fact, women do not have the hormonal potential for developing large muscles—strength, yes; large muscles, no. (2) The same reasons men train with weights are the same reasons women should train—to reduce the possibility of injuries and improve athletic performance. (3) The women who have been successful athletically without having participated in a strength-training program were successful not because they didn't lift, but *in spite of it.* In addition to these points, you might also stress that in the past few years, almost all top-level women athletes actively participate in organized strength-training programs, for example, Gayle Barron, Billie Jean King, and Marty Cooksey. By the way, I'm happy that your wife loves PowerWalking.

Q. Is there a minimal amount of time I should spend warming up before PowerWalking?
A. No specific "minimum" time guideline exists. You should, however, stretch each major muscle group and in so doing, stretch the musculature surrounding each major joint of the body. My advice to you is to stick to the basic rule of stretching: warm up at least until you break a sweat.

Q. At what age should a person start a regular weight-training program? I have a 12-year-old son who has expressed interest in weights. Is he too young? I also have access to a Universal Weight Machine. Would it be better to start him on this machine or with a set of free weights?
A. Twelve years old is *not* too young to start a person in a regular, properly supervised program of weight training. Although very little is known about weight training for children, the main danger, if there is one, arises from the stress that comes from the traditional practice of throwing and jerking

weights. Since this practice *would, could,* and *should* be prevented through proper supervision, your son would benefit from a properly organized and conducted lifting regimen. I personally believe it is better for people who are just starting a weight-training program to train on a machine (for example, Universal), which generally is safer for the weight lifter. Once a person learns *how* to train, he can switch to free weights if he desires. It is important to remember, however, that safety is a by-product to a great extent of *how* you use a tool, not just the design of the tool itself. A well-designed machine can easily injure someone who abuses the proper techniques for its use.

Q. What is a side ache and how can I prevent it?
A. Initially, when PowerWalking, your respiratory muscles are working anaerobically (without oxygen). When your system changes over to aerobic, there is a time lag in the redistribution of the blood, with not enough oxygen going to the diaphragm. At this point, some people suffer a "side ache." This is common in poorly conditioned persons or after a meal. A possible solution is to pick up the pace, forcing your system to reach maximum oxygen utilization faster. Another possibility is to hold your breath. A third technique is to pull with the thumb and forefinger at the point of discomfort.

Q. Will eating and drinking before PowerWalking affect my performance?
A. For the competitive athlete, eating before a game or contest can lower performance. Blood that could carry oxygen to the functioning muscles may be diverted to the muscles of digestion. Eating before PowerWalking should not, however, be a significant problem for most individuals. The feeling of discomfort associated with food in the stomach may be reason enough for some not to eat before PowerWalking. It is mostly psychological, however. The same is true for drinking. In fact, on a hot, humid day it may be essential for you to drink a glass of

water before going on a long PowerWalk. The body's fluids must be maintained. After PowerWalking, you should drink until you are no longer thirsty, then drink a little more.

Q. How does the principle of "demand" relate to PowerWalking and conditioning?
A. Demand refers to the principle that a system of the body must be stressed beyond its normal limits in order for there to be a substantial improvement. If a demand is not placed on a system, no improvement will occur in that system. For example, a person who can swim one mile will not improve the distance he can swim comfortably by swimming 100 yards. By the same token, a 5-minute miler will not break the 5-minute barrier by practicing 6-minute miles. Physiological responses occur within the body because of a particular need for that response. If you want to become more physically fit while PowerWalking, you need to PowerWalk at a level of intensity that places a demand on your systems, and periodically adjust your program to meet your body's capacity to handle higher demands.

Q. What is carbohydrate loading? Is it useful for a Power-Walker?
A. Carbohydrate loading is a technique in which athletes exercise vigorously several days before athletic competition while eating a low carbohydrate diet and then exercise lightly while eating a diet very high in carbohydrates approximately 48 hours prior to competition. Since this technique results in doubling the glycogen content of muscle, the "endurance potential" of the individual is greatly increased. The literature is unsure, however, about the values and potential risks associated with such techniques. To date, carbohydrate loading has been practiced to some extent by long-distance runners in an effort to maximize their "energy stores." Personally, I would not recommend such a technique for anyone.

Q. If I lift weights and develop more muscle, is there any chance that this newly developed musculature will turn to fat after I stop lifting weights?
A. The belief that unused muscle will somehow turn to fat is merely another of the unsubstantiated fairy tales that have persisted over the years. Muscle cannot under *any* circumstances turn to fat. If this were the case, an individual with a broken leg would find a blob of fat (in lieu of his leg musculature) once the cast was removed. In most instances, such a person will have experienced substantial atrophy (wasting away) of his leg. An unused muscle simply wastes away and eventually disappears. If you stop lifting weights, you'll simply return to your genetic "natural" state of muscular fitness.

Q. What factors should I consider when buying shoes for PowerWalking?
A. Most reputable authorities on the subject of purchasing shoes list the following eleven criteria, in order of priority:

1. Fit: Inside support for the arch and heel
2. Sole flexibility in the forward one third of the shoe
3. Cushioning to reduce shock
4. Heel lift to prevent strain on the back of the leg — ½" to ⅝" ideal
5. Adequate toe room
6. Heel width to prevent twisted ankles and knee injuries
7. Sole wear
8. Composition of uppers (Nylon is generally superior to leather.)
9. Weight (Don't sacrifice any of the above factors for lightness.)
10. Cost (Spend dollars on shoes, not on doctors.)
11. Color (Obviously, this should be the last consideration.)

Q. What are the symptoms of overtraining? Sometimes in my zeal to improve, I think I overtrain.
A. Several symptoms indicate that you might be overtraining. The severity and frequency of these symptoms varies from person to person. Included in the list of such symptoms are the following:

1. Muscle soreness
2. Headaches, sore throat, mild cold
3. Irritability
4. Problems falling asleep
5. Lack of interest in daily activities
6. Loss of appetite
7. Sudden drop in weight
8. Constipation or diarrhea
9. Skin eruptions

12

Make
Your Health
Your Top Priority

Recent surveys indicate that many Americans are not in the physical shape they should be. We've become a nation of spectators instead of participants. To a large extent, the blame for this situation lies in our daily habits and our exercise choices. How have we gone wrong?

It isn't too terribly difficult to see how changes in our daily habits over the years have adversely affected our level of fitness. There are many examples. To a large extent, the automobile has made walking obsolete in many situations. Television has replaced more strenuous pastimes. As the pace of life seems to grow even more hectic, junk food and fast food transfusions serve as quick-fix substitutes for nutritious meals. Time is the enemy. Convenience is the ally. Why walk through the snow when a snowmobile will get you there in half the time? Why take the time to fix a good meal when a burger and some fries will fill you up? The saga of physical self-destruction is almost endless.

In many instances, our choice of conditioning activities is almost as counterproductive as our daily living habits. Everyone is constantly looking for a gimmick or a fad—the *easy* way. In response to this demand, everywhere you turn there is another new diet, exercise gimmick, or conditioning tool— anything to make us appear younger, thinner, sexier, bigger, smaller, or better. Few people seem satisfied with approaching their health in a scientific manner. No matter how bad the economy, Americans will find a way to afford the luxury of beauty. Much of this is done through advertising that ranges from classy to just plain ridiculous. I especially love the "exercise" ads in magazines. A large, unattractive woman is shown with her hair untidy and her clothing too tight. The ad reads along the following lines: "Mrs. Jones looked like this just 10 weeks ago but after only 1½ weeks on this program, look at her now!" The second picture shows the same woman, only now she is gorgeous, dressed in a slinky outfit, hairdo from the Ritz, with a new man on her arm and, needless to say, an advancement in her career! As ridiculous as it may sound, people believe it! Whatever the price, the general public seems willing to pay unlimited amounts of money to appear handsome or beautiful.

People also seem to jump into any new activity promoting physical fitness as long as it appears that millions of others are doing the same and that the activity promises immediate results. The running craze is an excellent example of this. While jogging is an appropriate fitness activity for many people, for many others it isn't. Some people simply shouldn't run because of medical reasons. Others don't really enjoy running, but spend exorbitant sums of money on the best-looking running clothes or the latest pair of running shoes on the market. Within weeks (and sometimes sooner), these people quit running because they didn't enjoy it and, since they weren't committed to the required effort, they didn't achieve results. As an outgrowth of this scenario, many people have been "turned off" to exercise. This is extremely unfortunate.

The most important characteristic of PowerWalking is that *it works,* which can't be said about every conditioning program being extolled today. PowerWalking won't provide you with a magic way to get into shape while sitting on your duff—no program can do that. It won't tell you how to think yourself into great physical condition—because that can't be done. But if you want to improve your level of physical and mental well-being in the safest way possible and use the least amount of time, PowerWalking is for you.

I hope that after reading this book each of you will decide to make your health and fitness a top priority. PowerWalking is the tool that will enable you to achieve a physically fit body and a healthy outlook on life. The need is there. The way is clear. *Be the best that you can be!*

INDEX